TEN BOYS WHO MADE A DIFFERENCE

LIGHT KEEPERS

Irene Howat

CF4·K

Copyright © 2002 Christian Focus Publications
Reprinted 2003, 2004, 2005, 2006, 2007, 2008, 2016,
twice in 2017, 2019, 2020
Paperback ISBN: 978-1-85792-775-7
epub ISBN: 978-1-84550-842-5
mobi ISBN: 978-1-84550-843-2
Published by Christian Focus Publications Ltd,
Geanies House, Fearn, Tain, Ross-shire,
IV20 1TW, Scotland, Great Britain.
www.christianfocus.com
email:info@christianfocus.com
Cover design by Alister MacInnes
Cover illustration by Elena Temporin,
Milan Illustrations Agency.
Printed and bound in Turkey

All incidents retold in these stories are based on true situations. Where specific information about childhood incidents has been unobtainable the author has written these paragraphs using other information concerning family life, hobbies, home life, relationships freely available in other biographies as well as appropriate historical source material.

Cover illustration: This depicts Martin Luther as a young boy growing up in Germany. He lived in the area of Saxony where both his parents worked hard so that their son could not only have education, but have food and clothing and a roof over his head. Gathering wood for the fire, walking miles to get to the school room and then suffering lashes from the teacher's strap were all part of Martin Luther's normal school boy life before he went on to become one of the founders of the reformation.

For Samuel

Contents

Augustine of Hippo

Augustine raised his arm slowly in order not to frighten the birds roosting on the branch far above his head. Then he slid a stone into the leather band of his catapult, pulled back the cat gut and 'ping'. It flew through the branches and straight for the cluster of birds. There was a dull thud as one landed a short distance away. 'Gotcha!' said the boy. 'You'll roast nicely. Now let's see if we can find where the rest of your family moved to.'

Silently he slid among the undergrowth, taking care not to stand on any brittle twigs that might break and give him away. 'There they are!' he said to himself, seeing birds' shadows cast on to the ground by the bright North African sun. 'I'll try for a double,' he decided. From his leather pouch he took a little pile of stones, looking for two that would fit together in his catapult. They needed to be rounded on one side but flat on the other, and about the same size and weight. 'Perfect!' he whispered. 'These ones are ideal.' Again there was absolute silence until the 'ping,' but this time it was followed by two dull thuds.

Augustine unwound a length of thin creeper from the tree the birds had been on, broke it off and used it to tie together the legs of his three birds. 'Dad can have these two,' he thought. 'That should put him in a good mood.'

'It's me, Mum!' Augustine called as he neared home. There was silence. Dropping his birds on the floor, he went in quietly. It took a minute for his eyes to get used to the darkness after the brilliant sun. Seeing his mother on her knees didn't take him by surprise. Monica was a Christian, and when she wasn't doing all the work of an African mother, she was on her knees praying. Augustine listened. 'Lord, please forgive my child his sins. Please save his soul and use him to tell others about yourself,' she said.

'She's praying for me again as usual,' he thought, creeping back out into the sunlight. 'Maybe I'll become a Christian one day, but I'm too busy enjoying myself to be bothered just now. I wish Mum would stop asking God to convert me until I'm grown-up. It would be so easy to become a believer just to please her, but I want to please myself while I'm young.'

'I had a visit from a member of the Guard today, son,' Monica told her young son, when she joined him outside. 'There's been trouble, and they wondered if you were involved.'

Augustine looked at her. 'What am I meant to have done?' he asked, laughing just a little nervously. 'Because I didn't do it and I wasn't there when I did it.'

His mother looked serious. 'Augustine,' she said, 'I know you weren't involved because you were with me when the theft took place. But I also know that you don't always keep good company, and you do get into scrapes.'

Augustine hung his head, but just for a minute. 'I'm young, Mum,' he said. 'I'll not do anything so stupid that the Roman Guard will come for me. And I promise I will think about becoming a Christian ... sometime.'

'Sometime may not be soon enough,' his mother warned. 'Not everyone lives to grow up.'

A shiver went down the young boy's spine. 'But I will,' he said, defiantly.

'I'm not feeling well,' Augustine whined one day, not so long afterwards.

'What's wrong?' his mother asked. 'Are you feeling sick?' Before he could reply, he was caught in a spasm of pain. He was bent double with the force of it, and it was some minutes before he could speak. 'It's my stomach, Mum,' he said. 'I've got a terribly sore stomach.'

Monica felt his forehead. He was hot, and beads of perspiration were forming as she watched. Another spasm of pain hit him, and he landed on the floor. Within the hour he was tossing and turning. One minute he was roasting and the next he was shivering with cold. His mother washed him to bring his temperature down and gave him sips of water to drink.

'He's in a bad way,' said Patricius, Augustine's father. 'I've made an offering to the gods for him, but maybe you should be praying to your God too.'

'I've been praying to the Lord God for him since before he was born,' Monica said, 'and I've never stopped praying all of today.'

'I don't understand you Christians,' said Patricius. 'How do you expect your God to answer prayers unless you give him animal sacrifices?'

'Mother,' Augustine said weakly. 'I think I'm going to die.'

Monica looked at him and stroked his hand gently. 'Is he dying?' she wondered. 'He's not eaten for days and he's lost so much weight. He's just skin and bone.'

'Please, Mother,' he said, through tears. 'Please get the priest quickly. I want to go to heaven when I die.'

His mother kissed him, her tears mixing with his. 'I'll get the priest,' she said. But when she came back, not knowing whether her young son would be alive or dead, she discovered that he had made an amazing recovery! He was sitting up eating a piece of mango.

'Praise the Lord!' said the delighted Monica. 'Praise the Lord!'

'I don't think I'm going to die quite yet!' Augustine grinned.

Augustine loved his mother, but despite all that she had taught him, he grew up without becoming a Christian. And as if that wasn't bad enough, he went on to live an immoral life. Monica must have been deeply upset, but she kept on praying. Although she was proud of her son's able mind, and that he became a professor across the Mediterranean Sea in Italy, all she really wanted for him was that he should become a Christian. Patricius, who followed Roman gods and was not a Christian, didn't bother about his son's behaviour as that was how people lived in the Roman Empire.

One day in 386, when Augustine was thirty-two years old, he was walking along a road in the Italian city of Milan. He passed a beggar who was sitting on the pavement laughing. 'How can that man laugh?' he asked himself. 'He's sitting there on the street, owning nothing but the clothes he's wearing, and not even sure if he'll have a meal today, and he's happy. The man is laughing!' Augustine walked on. 'And here I am,' he thought. 'I've got a good job, another pretty girl, plenty of money, fine clothes and as much to eat as I want.' He stopped and looked back at the happy beggar. 'And I'm miserable,' he admitted. 'He's happy with nothing, and I'm miserable with everything. What a mess!'

'Would you like to come to church with me?' a friend asked him.

Augustine almost automatically said that he'd rather not, when he remembered the beggar. 'Yes, I'll come,' he said. 'I hear that Ambrose is a good preacher.'

'You can judge for yourself,' his friend commented. Monica, who had moved to Milan soon after her son, heard he was going to church and she prayed, how she prayed!

'He's a good preacher right enough,' Augustine said, as he and his friend left the church. 'I'm going to have to think about what he said.'

For some time he did just that. He wept over it too. 'I just can't take it in,' he told

Monica, one day. 'My sins are so terrible, how can God love me? How can Jesus have died for me after all that I've done?'

'Jesus died for us because we're sinners,' his mother explained. 'He wouldn't have needed to die if we'd been perfect. His blood was shed on the cross for you and for me, and because of that, our sins can be washed away.'

Soon afterwards Augustine was in his garden with a friend. He left his companion sitting under a tree and walked about restlessly. He was in a terrible mental muddle. He heard what sounded like a child's voice saying, 'Take it up and read it. Take it up and read it.' 'Is that a nursery rhyme?' he wondered, but couldn't remember any with those words. Suddenly he realised it was God speaking to him. He rushed back to his friend who had the Bible book of Romans. Opening it up, Augustine read words that told him he should look to Jesus and not live the immoral life he was living. Augustine suddenly knew the truth, confessed his sin and believed in Jesus. When he and his friend went back into the house, Monica learned that all her prayers had been answered.

Augustine became a great student of the Bible and teacher of the Christian faith.

Just eight years after he was converted, he was appointed Bishop of Hippo, the second most important town in North Africa. 'I'm happier now than I've ever been,' he told one of his friends. 'And it's all thanks to that happy beggar who made me realise how miserable I really was, and to my mother's prayers.'

'There is so much odd teaching,' his friend told him. 'Some people say that the Roman Empire fell because they stopped worshipping their gods. Others say that we go to heaven by living decent lives rather than by having faith in God. And there's a man called Pelagius who's teaching that we can be good; our only problem is that we choose not to be.'

'There are more strange teachers around as well,' said a priest who was with them. 'Have you heard of the Donatists?'

Augustine nodded. 'They've got some very funny ideas. They say that the church should be full of people who are absolutely good, that nobody who isn't as good as they are should be allowed in!'

'There's no hope for me then,' his friend said. 'I know myself well enough to know I don't belong in their kind of church.'

'We've got to get things sorted out,' the Bishop announced. 'Or nobody will know what Christians believe. They'll think Christianity is a religion that you can make up yourself – just believe in Jesus and add whatever you like to his life story.'

'I think God gave you such an amazing brain in order that you could think things through for us all,' Augustine's friend said. 'We're in such a terrible muddle.'

'With God's help I'll do what I can. And you,' he told his companion, 'must pray that I'll know the truth when I see it in the Bible and not accept one single teaching that is not in God's Word.'

'I hear that the Bishop's book is nearly ready,' was the news around Hippo in the year 400. Ten years later, the news was much the same. 'I hear that Augustine has written another book,' people said to each other. 'What a mind that man's got!' And the second book was not the last thing he wrote. The Bishop of Hippo spent much of his time studying wrong teachings, then searching the Bible to find out what was true.

'Augustine helped me straighten out my thinking,' a Christian said to his two companions, as they walked through the streets of Hippo in the year 421. 'After the evils of the Roman Empire, I'd been trying so hard to get my congregation to lead good lives that I was almost teaching the same things as Pelagius. How wrong I was to go that far! Of course God expects us to live decent lives, but we don't get to heaven by being decent. We are saved only by faith in Jesus. It doesn't matter how hard we try to be good, we can't be because we are sinners. I have to admit my teaching was not from the Bible. But now the Bishop has sorted me out.'

'And at last I've got an answer for the Donatists,' added their companion. 'Of course we shouldn't try to keep sinners from coming to church. After all, Jesus taught that weeds would grow among the crops till harvest time. That's what it's like in the church. There will always be non-Christians who come, and thank God for that because they might be converted. I'm grateful to the Bishop for making that clear.'

'We all owe a lot to Augustine, even the Romans,' the priest said. 'They thought it was because they'd stopped worshipping their gods that the Empire fell, but Augustine was able to show from the Bible that it was God's judgement, not their gods going in the huff! Maybe now some of them will come to believe in Jesus.'

'Wouldn't that be wonderful!' one of his friends smiled. 'That really would be good news.'

As they walked on, the priest seemed deep in thought. 'What's on your mind?' he was asked.

'I was just thinking how much Augustine has done for the Church. We were all in such a muddle until he came along. We didn't know the Bible and we didn't understand much of what we did know! I think the Church will remember Augustine hundreds of years from now, perhaps even thousands, because he's set us out on the right road.' 'You may be right,' laughed his friend. 'But we won't be here to see it!'

FACT FILE
Mediterranean Sea: The Mediterranean Sea lies between Europe and Africa. It is linked to the open ocean only by the narrow Strait of Gibraltar. It is more than 3,200 kilometres long and covers an area ten times the size of the United Kingdom.

Keynote: When he was young, Augustine and his friends often got into trouble. His mother realised that these friends were a bad influence on him. It is important to choose friends wisely. Ask God to help you make friends with people who trust and honour him. If your friends do not believe in Jesus, pray that God will help you to tell them about him and his love.

Think: Augustine's life before he became a Christian was immoral. He didn't follow God's rules. Look up Exodus chapter 20. Augustine wanted to disobey God's commands as he thought this was more fun. But it was when Jesus came into his life that Augustine's heart changed. What parts of your life need to change? Have you asked Jesus to take control of your life?

Prayer: Dear God, please help me to honour you in my life. Protect me from sin. I am sorry for the times that I displease you, but thank you for loving me and forgiving me. Amen.

Jan Hus

Jan Hus chose the stones carefully, five of them, about the same size and weight. Then he turned his back to the wind and threw them a few centimetres in the air. 'Can I catch all five?' he wondered, holding his breath. And he did. Next time he threw them a little higher and still caught them. Then he tried higher still and caught them again. 'This is fun,' he said to himself. 'I'll soon be good enough to take on the other boys at fives.' For days and days he practised on his own, until he could throw the stones about half a metre into the air and catch them more times than they fell.

'Where have you been?' his friends asked, when he joined them to play. Jan shrugged his shoulders. He didn't want to tell them he'd been practising fives. That was his secret until he was sure he was good enough.

'Want a game?' one of the boys said.

'What are you playing?'

'Just stones,' he said.

Jan smiled. 'Sure,' he agreed. 'I'll play.' He took his favourite stones from his pocket. The ones he needed were round pebbles, about the size of a blackbird's egg, and he always carried some with him. 'You draw and I start.' Jan took a chalky stone and drew a circle on the ground. He placed a larger pebble in the middle of the circle. 'That all right?' he asked. His friends said it was. All four boys stood in a line about two metres away and they took turns to throw into the circle. Each threw six stones.

'You win!' Jan told his friend. 'Your stone's the one nearest the middle. Let's play again.'

The afternoon passed very quickly because the boys were enjoying themselves so much.

'Jan! Jan!' a voice called from a short distance away.

Jan grabbed his stones and ran. 'I'll have to go,' he shouted over his shoulder. 'That's my mum.'

'Did you beat them at fives?' Mum asked, knowing her son had been practising.

'Not yet,' he grinned. 'I'll wait till I know I'm an expert before I play. I found another good stone today,' he added, holding up a blue pebble. 'You've been down at the river again,' smiled Mrs Hus. 'I used to collect coloured pebbles from the Blanice River when I was a girl. You could give that one to the saint,' she said.

Jan had a sinking feeling. He didn't want to give his stone to the statue of St John. But because he didn't want to upset his mother, he put it on the shelf in front of the carved statue. 'Oops!' he said. 'I nearly knocked it over!'

His mum's face turned white. 'For goodness' sake be careful,' she said anxiously. 'If you break the statue, we could have bad luck for years.' Jan looked at the shelf and wondered. The statue was made of stone; his blue pebble was a stone – could dropping one of them really bring bad luck?

While Jan was still a boy, his father died. All the village of Husinec came to his funeral Mass. The priest read prayers in Latin, and the Mass was said in Latin. There was not much that a boy could understand, and, because he was so upset, Jan needed to understand. After the burial he went back to the church. It was the only stone building there was, and it even had a bell tower. Usually Jan liked the sound of the bell, but when it rang on the day of his father's funeral, it gave Jan the shivers.

'Did you bow to the crucifix?' the priest asked, not unkindly, when Jan entered the church. Jan bowed to the stone figure of Jesus on the cross, then stood waiting to be spoken to.

'What do you want?' the priest asked.

'Please, Father,' Jan said, 'has my father gone to heaven?'

The priest looked shocked at the very idea. 'No,' he said. 'Your father was a good man but not that good. But if you ask the saints, perhaps he'll get to heaven one day.'

Jan felt a terrible emptiness, and when he looked at the statues of the saints all round the church, he wondered how speaking to carved and painted stones could possibly take his father to heaven.

'And remember to bow to the crucifix before you go.'

Hanging his head, he made the sign of the cross and bolted for the door.

'I can't possibly go to university, Mum,' a teenage Jan said, some years later. 'You don't have the money to send me.'

Mrs Hus folded her arms and stood firm. Jan realised his mother meant business! 'Just you listen to me,' she told him. 'A wealthy gentleman has agreed to pay for your education out of the goodness of his heart. You'll go to university and you'll study so hard that he'll be proud of you.' Her arms fell to her side, and Mrs Hus's face lost its fighting look. 'And I'll be proud of you too,' she added, smiling.

Soon afterwards, Jan took his small bundle of clothes and books and went off to Prague University.

'This is a beautiful place,' he said, as he walked round the city streets with another boy from the Blanice Valley.

'I've heard that it's the only place in Bohemia with stone buildings,' his friend said.

'And all these statues too,' Jan said. 'There is stone everywhere.' Jan remembered the games of fives he had played as a young boy at home and all the stones he collected at the river. 'I didn't collect enough stones to make a spire,' he smiled ... and then he remembered the blue pebble at the statue of St John. 'Do you believe that praying to statues can help you?' he asked his friend.

The other young man looked at him. 'If the Church says it, I believe it. Life's easier that way.'

There was a great buzz and worry in Bohemia. Jan was trying to work out why.

'Do you really think the world will come to an end at the turn of the century?' he asked an elderly friend. 'I can't see why 1st January, 1400 will be any different from 31st December, 1399.'

The elderly man shook his head. 'You're young,' he said. 'When you're as old as I am you'll take these things seriously. The Church wouldn't be asking for special collections to get us to heaven if they didn't think the world might end at midnight.'

Fear mounted as the year drew to its close. And as midnight on the last day of the year drew near, some people prayed to the saints, others drank themselves so drunk they didn't know what time of the year it was anyway, and some clung to their families and waited for the end. But it didn't come. Midnight passed, and the new century dawned.

By then Jan Hus was a university professor and in 1400 he became a priest. 'I'm having real problems,' he told his best friend. 'The more I hear of that Englishman Wycliffe's teaching, the less I like what the Church says.'

'So you say,' the other priest commented. 'But you don't explain the difference.'

The two young men sat down on the low branch of a tree. 'Right then,' Jan said. 'I'll try to explain some of the differences. The Church is rich and powerful. For example, who owns most of the land around here?'

'The Church,' his friend agreed.

Jan nodded. 'But surely Christians should give to the poor rather than collecting huge amounts of money for itself. I agree with Mr Wycliffe on that. Then there's another thing: this business of everything being in Latin. What good is that to the people of Bohemia?'

'True,' his friend said. 'But if the priests get the Mass and the prayers right, what does it matter if common people don't understand?'

'It matters because God wants them to know what they're doing. The Bible says that we should have boldness to come to God; there's no mention of going through a priest.'

'That's enough for now,' his friend said. 'My head's spinning with all your ideas.'

Jan Hus was not so easily put off. 'Hear me out,' he said, as they headed for home. 'Mr Wycliffe translated the Bible into English, and we should have it in our own language. And there's the Mass too. Why do we only get bread and no wine in the service? The Bible says that we've to take bread and wine in memory of Christ's death.'

His friend held up his hand. 'Enough is ENOUGH,' he said. 'You sound as though you believe the Bible more than the traditions of the Church!'

Hus grinned. 'I do,' he said. 'But I don't expect the Church to like it.'

Two years later Jan began to preach in the Bethlehem Chapel in Prague. 'I love this place,' he thought. 'It's not controlled by the Church. I can speak to people in their own language.'

Sunday by Sunday he preached in Czech, the congregations sang in Czech and God's Word was read in Czech too. At last the people were hearing the gospel in their own language.

'What a difference it makes when we understand the service!' people said, as they left the church.

'But do you think God hears our prayers when we don't pray first to the saints?' his rather worried companion asked.

'Jan Hus says that praying to a stone statue is no different from praying to a river pebble,' the first man commented. 'He told us that our prayers have to be offered through Jesus alone, not through the saints.'

'I'm not sure about that,' his friend said. 'I always pray to St Christopher when I'm travelling and ask him to keep me safe. I've a whole list of saints I pray to for different things, and I give money to them as well.'

Hus preached about Jesus, telling people that the Bible was the true Word of God and that God didn't tell lies. He explained that the Church had not always told the truth, and that it was still telling people what was wrong.

'How dare you say these things of the Church!' the Archbishop of Prague roared. 'How dare you tell people that the Pope is a mere man and a bad sinner at that – one that lies and deliberately misleads people!'

'I dare to say these things because I don't dare not to,' the pale, thin Jan Hus said. The Archbishop seemed huge next to him as he screamed his next question.

'What do you mean? Explain to me what you mean!'

Jan tried to explain about the Bible and about John Wycliffe, but the Archbishop was too angry to listen.

'Get out!' the furious man roared, his eyes bulging as though they would shoot out and hit Hus. 'You've not heard the end of this!'

The Archbishop of Prague gathered Wycliffe's books and any writings of Jan Hus and had them burned. Then he had Jan thrown out of the Church and banished from Prague.

'If he thinks he'll stop me preaching,' Hus told his friends, 'he's wrong. If I can't preach in the town, I'll preach in the villages. And if he chases me out of the villages, I'll preach on the hillsides and by the rivers of Bohemia.'

As more and more people followed Jan Hus's teaching rather than listening to what the priests had to say, the Archbishop planned how to get rid of him. Even the Pope wanted him out of the way.

'You're not safe anywhere,' a friend told Jan one day in 1414. And he was right. Hus was arrested and thrown into prison. That winter he was taken to Gottlieben Castle, where he was put in a draughty tower, bound hand and foot and left to freeze.

'Dear Jesus,' he prayed, as he sat propped against the stone wall of the tower, 'thank you so much that you're right in this place with me. Please forgive those who have put me here, poor misguided people who think that if the stone I'm leaning against was carved into the shape of a saint it could answer their prayers! Heavenly Father, show them the truth, show them that the Bible is true.'

The winter passed; spring came, then summer. The tower was less draughty, but his jailors were no more kind. In July the

Archbishop sent for him. Jan was taken out of the tower, dragged down the steep stairs, then out into the morning sunshine.

'My beautiful land,' he thought, enjoying the sight of it, and knowing he would soon see an even more beautiful land than Bohemia.

A stake was hammered into the ground and Hus was chained to it. He watched as a bonfire was built around him. Jan saw the lighted torch arrive and the first sparks of the fire fly in the air. He felt the heat come nearer and said before the flames engulfed him, 'The aim of all my preaching, teaching, writing and actions has been to turn people from their sins. And that teaching I seal with my death today.'

As he finished speaking, the flames roared around him. The people who stood by the fire thought they were watching Jan Hus burn. But only his body was there. His soul was in that better land; it was in heaven with the Lord Jesus.

FACT FILE
Prague: This used to be the capital of Czechoslovakia. It is now the capital of the Czech Republic as Czechoslovakia has separated into two countries – the other being Slovakia. Before Czechoslovakia existed, this country was called Bohemia. Prague, which is sometimes called The City of 100 Spires, was built in a broad valley along the banks of the River Vlatva. The traditional heart of the city is the cobbled Old Town Square which is dominated by a monument to Jan Hus.

Keynote: Jan Hus believed that we should have a boldness when dealing with God. We shouldn't feel afraid to pray to God. We can bring all our problems and cares to our loving heavenly Father. The apostle Peter in 1 Peter 5:7 says that we should cast all our cares on God who cares for us. You don't have to ask someone else to speak to God for you.

Think: Jan's main aim in life was to turn people away from their sins and to bring them to know the Lord Jesus Christ for themselves. How has sin harmed your life and the world around you?

Prayer: Dear God, turn me away from my sin towards you and help me to know Jesus Christ for myself. Teach me to pray to you and cast all my cares on you. Make my main aim in life to praise you and enjoy you forever. Amen.

Martin Luther

Martin peered round the corner of a road in Mansfield in Saxony. 'Are there any goblins coming?' his brother asked from behind. He was younger than Martin and quite happy to let his older brother go first, especially in the dark.

'No,' whispered Martin. 'I think it's safe.' But even though he sounded confident, he was shaking and every bit as scared as his brother.

'What's that!' he screamed, when something touched his leg.

'It was a cat,' the other boy said. 'I thought you'd seen it coming.'

'I don't want to go past the church,' Martin announced. 'We'll go home the long way.'

'I don't like going past the church either,' his brother agreed. 'There are spirits there, and they sometimes run away with children, especially boys.'

'Who told you that?'

'That's what someone told a gang playing near the church. He said that spirits took boys away to work for them, and that they could never get back out of the underworld. They're held prisoners for ever and ever and ever.'

'I think that's nonsense,' the older boy said, but he decided never to go near the church on his own just in case. He didn't want to risk being a prisoner in the underworld.

As he lay in bed that night, Martin thought about goblins and churches, about spirits and priests. Somehow he couldn't separate them out.

'I wish there weren't so many things to be afraid of,' he thought. 'The priest scares me most of all because he says boys are bad and can't go to heaven and that they sometimes spend hundreds of years in purgatory.'

'What is purgatory?' he asked his father the following day.

'It's where we go when we die,' the man explained. 'And we are there until we can go to heaven.'

'But I want to go straight to heaven when I die,' Martin said.

'You'll not do that, son,' Mr Luther said, sadly. 'You've already done too many bad things. Only those who live nearly perfect lives go to heaven right away. And

I suppose they are all Popes and Cardinals and Archbishops.'

'What about bishops and priests?' asked Martin. His father shook his head.

'I expect most of them will go to purgatory.'

Martin was near to tears when he asked, 'How do you get out of purgatory?'

'When people who are still alive say enough Masses or give enough money to the church,' was the upsetting answer.

'Are you awake?' his brother asked.

'Yes.'

'What are you thinking about?'

Martin told his young brother his thoughts, but this only made his young brother ask more questions. 'What happens if families don't say enough Masses? Do people have to stay in purgatory for ever?'

'I suppose so,' Martin said.

'But what if Mum died and Dad was killed down the mine and there was nobody to say Masses for us?'

Because Martin was beginning to feel really quite scared, he decided to pretend he'd fallen asleep and not heard what his brother had said. He grunted, turned round, and lay awake for hours thinking. 'I wonder if we've said enough Masses for my baby brothers and sisters who've died?' he found himself worrying. 'Maybe they're still in purgatory?'

The next morning Martin was slow to get up and his father was not at all pleased. 'You're a lazy, lazy boy!' he said, taking the leather belt off his trousers. 'I've worked hard for you, and all you can do is sleep. When we came to Mansfield, we had hardly a penny. I worked my fingers to the bone to feed and clothe you. I work so hard that I own the mine now. And what do I get? An eldest son who can't get out of his bed in the mornings!'

Martin knew better than to dodge his father's belt, so he took his punishment without flinching. 'Go and help your mother gather wood,' Mr Luther said, as he put on his belt again.

Martin waited until he was out of sight of his home before rubbing where his father's belt had hit him. But he didn't risk stopping long for he knew his father would come after him to check what he was doing. He guessed where his mother would be in the forest because a large tree had blown down and there was plenty of wood to be had from it.

'You've come to help,' his mother said, when she saw him.

'Dad sent me,' Martin told her. 'But I would have come anyway.' He enjoyed collecting wood for the fire. 'Do you know something, Mum. Wood heats you up twice.'

'What do you mean?' his mother asked.

Martin explained. 'It heats you up the first time when you're gathering it and it heats you up again when it burns on the fire!'

'You're an intelligent boy,' the woman said. 'No wonder your father wants you to go to school.'

It was such a long walk to school that, at first, Martin was carried part of the way there.

'What's school like?' his younger brother asked him in bed when they had time to talk.

'It's been a terrible week,' Martin explained. 'The teacher is so cross. He saves up beatings all week and gives them on a Friday. I got fifteen lashes today.'

'That must have been sore,' his brother said sympathetically.

'Why do you think I'm lying on my side?' Martin spat. 'The teacher says I'm so bad that I'll never get to heaven.'

That was the beginning of another sleepless night, and it wasn't just because he was sore from the beating.

After school Martin went on to study at university.

'I'll be a lawyer,' he told his father, 'and you'll be proud of me.'

But a thunderstorm changed his plans. While he was studying law, he went out riding one day, and a furious storm suddenly crashed right overhead. Lightning forked this way and that, blinding in its brightness.

'Help me St Anne!' a terrified Martin cried, 'and I'll become a monk.' He did survive and he did become a monk, though his father was not best pleased.

But even though he was a monk, the fear of spending for ever in purgatory still plagued the young Luther.

'What can I do to make myself good enough for heaven?' he asked himself over and over again, until his mind was nearly bursting.

'I'll say the Lord's Prayer fifty times each morning,' or 'I'll only eat one small meal each day,' or 'I'll wear the scratchiest horsehair vest I can find,' or 'I'll get up at two each morning and pray until daylight,' he thought, and tried them all.

He even went to Rome where he found a building that was supposed to be Pilate's house. When he reached it, Martin got down on his knees, crawled up the twenty-nine steps and stopped to pray on each of them.

'It doesn't matter what I do,' he wept afterwards. 'Nothing makes me feel as though I'll escape purgatory.' He was nearly out of his mind with worry.

One day, while Luther was studying, an amazing idea dawned on him. 'Can this be true?' he said to himself, absolutely brain-blown at what he was thinking. 'Can it possibly be true that we are saved by faith and not by works?'

He went from verse to verse in his Bible, shaking with excitement. Tears of sheer relief flowed down his face. He brushed them off impatiently because they were stopping him reading the Bible!

'It's true!' he said softly. He slid from his high stool and nearly fell. His legs were wobbly with relief, and he felt as though he had lost half his weight. 'It's as if I've been carrying a huge burden that's suddenly gone.'

Sitting down, he thought through what he'd discovered. Had anyone come into the room, they would have wondered what had happened. The serious monk, Martin Luther, was one minute wiping tears from his eyes, and the next jumping up to look at his Bible, then sitting down and smiling more broadly than he had done for years, then striding about saying over and over again, 'It's true! Praise the Lord, it's true!'

Over the months that followed his discovery, Martin did a great deal of studying and thinking.

'The Bible absolutely clearly says that we are saved by faith in God,' he said to himself. 'So why is it that I studied and worried for years and didn't see the truth?'

The answer to that question really upset him. 'I didn't see the truth because the Church has taught me lies all of my life.'

Luther shook his head at the thought then thumped his desk with his fist. 'Every day of my life I've worried about how I'd get out of purgatory and now I discover that there is no such place! It's not in the Bible at all!' He strode about the room, thinking aloud. 'Why has the Church lied? Why? Why? There can only be one reason – that it wanted everyone to be afraid, that it wanted to control us through fear.' His eyes blazed. 'And it's still doing it! What am I to do?'

In 1517 there was an announcement made in Luther's church, and in every other church as well. 'The church of the Holy Father, the Pope, is to be rebuilt. As this will cost a great deal of money, the Holy Father has most graciously decided that there will be a sale of indulgences. Anyone buying an indulgence will have their sins or a loved one's sins forgiven and will therefore go to heaven.'

Martin heard this with astonishment. His head spun as he left the building. 'What's an indulgence?' he asked himself. 'It's only a piece of paper saying your sins are forgiven. How can people believe that by paying money for a piece of paper, God will take them to heaven? Surely ordinary people will have more sense than to believe that.'

Suddenly he stopped, shocked. 'No! They won't! They'll do just what I did for years. They'll believe it because the Church says it. That's terrifying. People will pay out money they can't afford to go to a heaven they'll never see!'

Luther spent a long time in his study preparing a document he knew would cause a storm. When he'd finished writing, he'd made up a list of 95 ways in which the Church's teaching was not from the Bible, most of them to do with purgatory and indulgences. He took the long sheet of paper, some nails and a small hammer and set out for the Castle Church in his town of Wittenberg.

When he arrived at the church door, he didn't go in. Instead, he nailed the list to the door. News of what he had done soon spread through the town.

'I wonder if Luther's right,' one or two people said.

'How dare he say that the money we've spent on indulgences won't take us to heaven!' others fumed.

And a number worried and wept because they just didn't know what to think.

Before long, news of what Martin had done reached the Pope who was not at all pleased with his monk. 'Bring him here!' he demanded. 'There'll be trouble if people listen to what he's saying. Bring him here and I'll sort him out.'

When the Pope's order arrived, Martin Luther refused to go to Rome. 'There's no such person as a Pope in the Bible,' he told a friend, 'and we're certainly not told to obey a man rather than God. So the Pope can say what he likes, but I'm not jumping to attention and obeying him!'

'That's dangerous thinking,' his friend said seriously. Then he smiled. 'But it's true, splendidly true. For so long the Church has lived in fear of Popes, and now we can be free from them.'

As Luther's teaching became well known, people began to gather round him, who already thought as he did. Some had been influenced by an Englishman called John Wycliffe who had lived over a hundred and fifty years before Luther. Nearer home, Jan Hus had made the same discovery in Prague a century later. Followers of Wycliffe and Hus were encouraged that Martin Luther stood up strongly for Bible truths. And some of them were among a group of people who met with Martin on 10th December, 1520, for a bonfire.

Having gathered together many books of Church teaching, which they knew to be untrue, they burned them publicly.

'The Church has led us far from the truth,' one man, who was enjoying the sight of the burning books, said to his neighbour, 'and change has been brewing quietly for years. But it will come soon now. I believe tonight marks a big step in the process of reformation.'

'What is reformation?' his son asked.

'It's change, son,' his father said. 'It's the change that will come as we read the Bible rather than listen to the wrong things the Church has been teaching.'

The fire blazed brightly as book after book was thrown on. And the glow reflected on the faces of those who had the courage to stand near it.

'There's an excitement in their faces,' Luther thought, 'and there's joy too – the joy of being free of the fear of purgatory and sure of the hope of heaven.'

FACT FILE
Rome: Rome is believed to have been founded in 753 B.C. and it has been the capital of a united Italy since the year 1871. The dome of St Peter's, built in 1590, still dominates the skyline. In the year 2016 Rome had a population of 2,869,461.

Keynote: A belief in purgatory is a mistaken belief. When people die, they either go to heaven or hell. There is no place where people go to be purified from sin. It is the blood of Jesus Christ that cleanses us from all sin. His death on the cross means that all who trust and love him will have eternal life and go to be with him as soon as they die.

Think: The Bible says that we are saved by faith and not by works. Martin Luther discovered this and was overjoyed. Think about how perfect Jesus is, yet he had to die to free us from our sins. What does this tell you about sin? It tells you how awful it is. Think how impossible it would be for us as sinful people to ever do anything good enough to get to heaven. Only faith in Jesus saves.

Prayer: Dear God, protect me from wrong beliefs. Give me a clear understanding of what you say in your Word, the Bible. Thank you for sending the perfect Lord Jesus, your only son, to die for me on the cross. Help me to trust in him. Amen.

Ulrich Zwingli

Ulrich, who was aged just five, sat at the table with his father. 'There are hundreds of Zwinglis in the world,' he said.

His father smiled. 'Yes, I suppose there are,' he laughed. 'But mostly they live near here. The area around Wildhaus is the Zwingli part of Switzerland. There are different family names in other parts of the country.'

His face suddenly saddened. 'Do I need to go away to Uncle Barthelemy's in another part of Switzerland?' he asked.

Mr Zwingli straightened his back. 'Yes,' he said firmly, 'you do; and for the very last time I'll explain why. With a houseful of children there's no chance for you to have a good education, and I think you're clever enough and that you'll take to studying and do well in the world.'

'But I'll miss my brothers and sisters, and mother,' he said, then added quickly, 'and you too.'

'You're going, and that's an end of it. As soon as the snows have melted, I'll take you to your uncle.'

Ulrich knew better than to argue with his father. He wasn't the kind of person who lost an argument with his children.

'Will you come and play snowballs?' his brother asked the following morning. Ulrich didn't know whether to enjoy what was left of his time at home or to start feeling sad about leaving, even though the snow was still thick. He decided to enjoy himself.

'You're on!' he said. 'The best snow for snowballs is in the meadow.' The boys ran to the meadow, snow slowing them down as it got deeper. 'I really am going away,' Ulrich told his little brother.

The four-year-old's eyes lit up. 'That's exciting!' he said. 'You'll have lots of adventures. And I'll have the bed all to myself.'

'I don't think so,' the older boy said. 'I think Mother's having another baby.'

April came and the snow began to melt. Mrs Zwingli packed a bag of clothes for her son and presents for the family he was to stay with. Ulrich noticed that his mother looked sad when she was doing his packing, and that made him want to cry.

'You'll like your uncle,' she told him. 'He's a priest and a kind man.'

'Kind?' Ulrich wondered exactly how kind he was. 'Perhaps he won't have a wooden stick like Father's one.'

The bag lay packed and ready for the last of the snow to go. 'We're leaving tomorrow,' his father said, as Ulrich went to bed one night. Ulrich turned to his father, 'But ...'

'No buts,' was the firm reply.

For five years Ulrich lived with his uncle. He was a good man and a good teacher. Ulrich showed everyone that his father was right, for he was clever and he did enjoy studying. Ulrich was especially good at music and could easily have become a professional musician.

'I think you should send the boy to school in Basle,' Uncle Barthelemy told Ulrich's father, when his nephew was ten years old. Five years later, having done very well in Basle, his teacher there recommended to Mr Zwingli that the boy should do even more studying in Berne. But first there was some time to enjoy being back at home.

Ulrich and his friends pulled their wooden sledges up the best slope on his father's farm. 'You go first,' Zwingli shouted. 'And I'll see if I can follow in your sledge tracks.'

The youngest boy went first, then the other. They landed in a heap at the bottom of the hill. 'Watch out, you two!' Ulrich yelled, using his new launching technique. It involved placing his sledge hard against the trunk of a tree then lying flat on it and pushing his feet against the tree trunk with as much force as he could produce. He went off like a stone from a sling. 'Here I come!'

The two at the bottom looked up and saw their friend's sledge almost flying down the slope towards them. They scrambled out of the way only just in time. Ulrich was moving too fast to come to a controlled stop. Instead, he rammed their two wooden sledges, parted company with his own and landed some distance in front. Even then he didn't stop but went on slithering down the hillside. When he eventually came to a halt and clambered back up to his friends, his eyes were shining with excitement and his nose pouring blood. 'That's what I call sledging!'

The older of his two friends looked him in the eye and said, 'That's what I call stupid.'

'What a mess you're in,' Mrs Zwingli told the teenager, when he arrived back home covered in blood. 'Were you like this when you were away studying?'

Ulrich's eyes twinkled as he thought of some of the mischief he'd got up to, the scrapes he'd found himself in, and the fights he'd fought and won. There had been several bleeding noses over the years, and they were not always his!

'You'll have to behave more like a man now that you're going to university in Vienna.' That night Ulrich wrote in his diary, '1498, I must behave more like a man and less like a child.'

By 1506, Zwingli was back in his native Switzerland and working as a priest. For several years he worked away quietly, all the while becoming aware that there were things in the Church of his day that were far from right. 'We must trust in Christ rather than the Church,' he told his congregation. 'The Church is made up of sinful human beings, and it can and does make mistakes, but Christ is the sinless Son of God.'

'You're looking tired,' his friends often told him. 'And you've got bags under your eyes.' 'I don't know why you need to study so much. After all, you've been to two universities.'

Ulrich laughed. 'I study because I both want to and need to. I want to know Greek so I can study the New Testament in the language in which it was written,' he explained.

'But that doesn't seem to do you any good,' the friend pointed out. 'The more you study the Bible, the more unsettled you become.'

'What's on your mind now?' Zwingli's friend asked, realising he wanted to talk.

'It's the Mass,' he began. 'The Church teaches us that the bread and wine in the Mass actually become the body and blood of Jesus; that we actually eat a piece of the Lord's real body and drink some of the Lord's real blood. That is a grotesque teaching.'

'It bothers me too,' his friend, Gunter, said. 'But go on.'

'The bread and wine are just signs of his body and blood, otherwise we're cannibals! The thought makes me ill.'

'We're on dangerous ground,' his friend said. 'We're going to have to be careful.'

'Have you heard of Martin Luther?' someone asked Zwingli in 1519.

'No,' Ulrich replied. 'Who's he, and why should I have heard about him?'

'Read this,' Gunter said, giving him a book by Luther. That night Zwingli read until his candle died, then he lit another, and another. 'This book says just what I think,' he told himself, when the last candle had guttered and he was so tired he didn't have the energy to go for a fourth one. 'But he's a braver man than I am. I'll have to give this some serious thought.' Although he was exhausted Ulrich didn't sleep a wink that night.

The following morning he started reading Luther's book even before he had his breakfast, and by late that afternoon he'd finished it. His mind was in a whirl. 'I'm going to give this to Gunter to read then we can talk all about it.'

It was a week later that the two men settled in front of a log fire in Ulrich's home. They had Luther's book and their Bibles on a table in front of them. 'What do you think?' Zwingli asked.

His friend looked serious. 'This Luther is right,' he said. 'The Church is in a mess. Cardinals and archbishops care only about their own power and many of them are living very wicked lives. The Pope is selling indulgences; telling people all they've got to do to go to heaven is pay up to the Church.'

'The question is,' Ulrich said, 'can we go on as we are, or should we stand up and be counted, like Luther has?'

Zwingli shook his head. For three years he made no decision, but more and more often he found himself preaching against the teachings of the Church.

In May 1522, Ulrich sat down to write to a university friend. 'You'll find it difficult to believe what I'm going to tell you,' he began, 'but I promise you it's true. As you know the Church teaches that we should eat fish rather than meat for four weeks before Easter. Well, some friends and I were at a meeting at a printer's house. We were working on printing part of the New Testament. The printing press had been going day and night for weeks, and the workmen were tired and hungry. The printer's wife bought some sausages because fish was so expensive. She brought in the dish of sausages ... and the smell was delicious! My mouth was watering. But, on with the story ... I didn't eat any but the other men there did, so disobeying the Church's teaching. Although I didn't have any, after I'd thought about it, I decided that there was nothing at all in the Bible about eating fish rather than meat, and that's what I told my congregation.

'Now, you'll never believe what happened. The men who ate the sausages were fined and some of them put in prison!

'That's the last straw as far as the Church is concerned. Since I've read Luther's books, I'm really admiring his courage. Now I've no choice but to break with the Pope.'

'It's so different for us than for Luther,' Zwingli said, when he and his friends were discussing things in the autumn of the following year. 'Our town council is quite happy for us to preach the Gospel of Christ rather than the teachings of the Church. We've such a lot to be grateful for.'

'And have you heard the news?' one of the men said. 'The Council says that all idols have to be taken from churches, and all the bits and pieces of wood that the Church says are from Christ's cross, and the fragments of bone that are meant to be from saints' skeletons. Organs have to go too. But the Council says it has all to be done in an orderly way and without any riots.'

Zwingli wiped his forehead. 'I can hardly believe it!' he said. 'It seems that the Reformation in Switzerland is going to be quite a peaceful affair.'

Not everyone in Switzerland was convinced by Zwingli and his fellow Reformers. Parts of the country seemed to become even more keen on the Roman Church as the Reformation continued. At first there were occasional skirmishes between Romanists and Protestants, but it wasn't long before things became more serious. Catholic armies formed, and Protestant troops gathered too. A peace treaty was drawn up, but it was soon broken.

'What are we going to do?' Zwingli's friends asked him, as they met to talk about the problem.

Ulrich looked surprised that the question was asked. 'What do you mean? We'll get our swords and fight for the truth!'

There was silence in the room. 'Is that the right thing to do?' someone asked.

Taking a deep breath Zwingli began, 'There is right and wrong here, and we are on the side of right. Romanists have gathered their armies and they are ready to advance. Do you hear what I'm saying?' he insisted. 'They are ready to advance, to go into Protestant areas where they will clamp down on the people like never before. We've been holding communion services; they'll change it back to the Mass. They'll insist that people believe they're eating and drinking Jesus' body and blood. Will you not fight for that?' The room was absolutely silent.

Zwingli waited a minute then went on. 'The Pope will force indulgences on poor people. Cardinals and archbishops will grasp back the power they lost, and our people will become slaves once again, slaves to the Church, slaves to superstition and slaves to fear. Are you willing to let that happen? Are you willing to take up your swords for what's right?'

'You might be killed, Ulrich,' someone said.

Zwingli's eyes shone. 'I've shed my blood for fun in the snow. I've shed my blood for the sake of mere arguments when I was young. Do you expect me to be afraid of shedding my blood for the truth of Christ?'

In October 1531, the Romanist army invaded Protestant Zurich. Zwingli was true to his word and fought in the defending army. He fought for what he believed to be true and was killed. But Ulrich did not die in vain as Switzerland went on to play a huge part in the Reformation. Some of his friends felt he should not have gone into battle, rather he should have found a peaceful way of spreading the good news of Jesus. But all of them had to agree that their dead friend had lived up to his motto, 'Do something bold for God's sake!'

FACT FILE
Books: These are an excellent invention. Everything we know and all the thoughts and ideas of human beings may be found in books. The Egyptians were writing books in 2500 B.C. on a type of paper made from a reed called papyrus. These books were made on long strips which were rolled up round a stick when not being read. The Romans were the first to make books like those we know today... but they were still written by hand on parchment. It was not until printing was invented in the 15th century that more than one copy of a book could be made at a time.

Keynote: When Christians take communion, the bread and wine are eaten to remind them of what Jesus did on the cross. They are what we call symbols. Nothing happens to the bread and wine. The most important thing has already happened. Jesus Christ died to save us from our sins and has risen from the dead, victorious.

Think: The church is made up of people who sin. When people become Christians, their sins are forgiven but they are still sinners. Loving and trusting in Christ is just the beginning of God's work in their lives and hearts. Christians hate the sin that they do but they are not totally free of sin until they die and go to heaven. Do you hate sin? Are you upset and ashamed when you disobey God? Do you wish you were more like Jesus? Do you wish you loved Jesus more? These are signs of someone who is a real Christian and is a follower of the Lord Jesus Christ.

Prayer: Father God, thank you for everything you give me. Thank you for your Word, the Bible, and for the gift of reading. Thank you that your word tells me the truth about my sin and how you want to save me from it. Amen.

William Tyndale

William loved the noise of his mother making butter. She sat beside the wooden churn and turned the handle round and round, then round and round again, for what seemed a very long time to a very small boy.

To start with, there was the swish and splash of milk each time the wooden paddle turned inside the churn. Then the sound changed to a gloop, gloop, gloop.

'That's the milk thickening,' his mother had explained, and, because he was brainy and intelligent, William never forgot it. As the gloops became slower, his mouth watered. Then, all of a sudden, the gloops stopped, and there was a quiet thud. William knew exactly what had happened. The milk had separated into butter and milky water that would be used in his mother's baking. She called it buttermilk.

'May I?' he asked, grinning at his mother. She knew exactly what he meant and she opened the churn and let him take some of the newly made butter on his finger. 'It's lovely,' he said, licking his lips. 'Our cow's milk makes the best butter in all of Gloucestershire.'

When Mrs Tyndale had made the butter into a neat pat, she poured off the butter-milk that was left and started her baking. William sat down to watch.

'Don't you want to go out and play with your brothers?' his mother asked.

'No,' he said. 'I want to watch you and ask you questions.'

'There was never a boy like you for questions,' the woman laughed, 'though often it's only poor answers I can give you. What is it you want to know today?'

Screwing up his face seemed to make questions come into his mind, so that's what William did, and a question was suddenly there!

'What year is it?' asked the eight-year-old.

'It's the year of our Lord 1502.'

'Why do you say the year of our Lord?'

Mrs Tyndale was used to his questions and patient in answering them. 'That's because we count the years from the time of the birth of the Lord Jesus Christ.'

'Who decided we'd do that?'

'Important men in the church did that many years ago.'

'What kind of important men?'

This was getting difficult! 'The Pope and his bishops and archbishops,' his mother explained.

'Were all the bishops in Gloucestershire there to decide it?' the child asked. Mrs Tyndale explained that the bishops in Gloucestershire had not been born when the years were first numbered.

As they were talking, the woman had kneaded her bread, and it was ready to be put somewhere warm to rise. She sat down for a minute to rest.

'Why is it that the bishops and priests use Latin in church?' her son asked. 'I only understand little bits of what they are saying.'

His mother smiled. 'Then you understand more than I do,' she said. 'You seem to have a real gift for other languages.'

William grinned. 'I know some French. The soldier who came to Slimbridge taught me some of his words.'

'Yes, I remember that,' Mrs Tyndale said. 'But sitting here with you won't get the work done. Off you go and play with your brothers.'

'One more question. Please.' His mother nodded. 'Why do we use Latin in church and not our own language?'

'That's just how it is,' the patient woman explained. 'Though it would be easier on all of us if we knew what was being said.'

The older William grew, the more difficult his questions became for his mother. Even his father had problems answering many of them. His brothers Edward and John sometimes teased him, telling him that his brain would burst if he knew the answers. The questions William asked changed as he grew up, but there was one for which he could not find an answer that pleased him.

'Why do we have to believe what the priests tell us when we could read the Holy Book for ourselves if we had it in our own language? They could be talking rubbish for all we know.'

'Shh,' his father hissed. 'When it comes to saying things like that, the very walls have ears. I've told you over and over again that if you want to discuss these things, we must do it out in the fields where there's no chance of being overheard.'

William was around fifteen and just about to go to Oxford University. 'Can we go for a walk then, Father? I need to talk.'

Both wrapped cloaks about themselves as there was a nip in the autumn air. And they set out to walk and talk.

'Why is the Holy Book not in English?' William asked, when he was sure nobody was within earshot.

'It was once,' his father explained. 'Around a hundred years ago a man named John Wycliffe translated the Bible from Latin into English. But the bishops didn't like that because they thought that if people had God's Word in their own language, the Church would no longer have power over them.'

'Have you ever seen Wycliffe's translation?' William asked.

'No. Even though they took hundreds of hours to write out by hand, if any copies were found, they were burned.'

'What!' William was full of rage at the thought. 'How dare they do that!'

'Keep your voice down,' his father said. 'And for goodness' sake be careful what you say when you go to university. People have been burned for saying such things.'

While William was a student in Oxford, he discovered for himself what it meant to be a Christian. And it was no easy thing in those days. After he finished his studies, he became chaplain to a family, and teacher of their two sons. It was while he was doing that for a living that he decided to do something much more interesting with his life ... and very much more dangerous.

William Tyndale decided to translate the Bible into English. And rather than using the Church's Latin Bible, he made up his mind to translate it all from the original Greek and Hebrew languages. 'Mother always said I was good at languages,' he thought. 'I'm going to have to be!'

'It's a terrible thing,' a friend told him, sometime later. 'But if you are serious about translating the Bible into English, you're going to have to go abroad to do it. You'll be found and killed if you stay here.'

'Do you really think so?'

'Have you not heard the news the coachman brought this morning?' his friend asked. William shook his head. 'Seven people have been burnt at the stake for teaching their children the Lord's Prayer, the Ten Commandments and the Apostles' Creed in English.'

'I've no choice then but to go to Germany. Surely I'll get peace there to do the job.'

'And while you're at your translating, there will be people here in England praying that by the time it's finished, God's Word will be able to be read in English here in England.'

By 1525, Tyndale had translated the whole of the New Testament. He wrote to his friend in England telling him the good news. So that no one reading the letter would know what it was about, he used a code that the two of them made up before he left for Germany.

'Listen to this,' his friend told a small group of Christians who had met to pray. 'William says that the first copies should be here within a few months. Isn't that wonderful! The invention of the printing press has made such a difference. It means that copies can be made quickly, not like in the days of Wycliffe when everything had to be written out by hand.'

'How will it be distributed?' someone asked.

'It will have to be from Christian to Christian because if the Church finds out about it, they'll burn any copies they find.'

However, the Church authorities in England did get wind of what was going on, and people were sent to Europe to look for Tyndale. As they travelled from country to country, they bought any Protestant books they could find and burned them all! The King of England also sent spies to look for him. They found Tyndale, but they couldn't persuade him to return to England with them.

'Tell me why I should go back with you,' he demanded of them.

'It's your duty as an Englishman to obey the King's orders,' he was told.

'And is it the duty of an English court to try me and put me to death for giving people God's Word in a language they can read for themselves?'

'Why do you think you'd be put to death?' one of the king's agents asked.

Tyndale heaved a sigh. 'Do you think I don't know that copies of my New Testament are publicly burned? Do you think I don't know that those who trust in the Lord Jesus rather than the Roman Church are tied to a stake, that a bonfire is built around them and they are burned to death? Do you really think that because I'm not in England I don't know what's happening to God's people there?'

The king's agents gave up and, as they left Tyndale's home, one said to the other, 'I don't know where he gets his information, but he certainly knows what's going on at home!'

By 1529, Tyndale had translated several books of the Old Testament from Hebrew into English, but the manuscript was lost in a shipwreck. But by the following year a replacement had been made with the help of his assistant, Miles Coverdale, and smuggled into England.

'I can hardly believe that I'm holding God's Word and can read it for myself,' a new Christian said. 'Look here: it says, "You shall not kill". I don't understand how the Church can kill Christians when the Bible says, "You shall not kill".'

'You know you're risking your life being a believer,' an old Christian man told him.

'If you're caught carrying out your plan, you'll get no mercy.'

The young Christian, his eyes glowing with enthusiasm, shook his head. 'I'm a sailor,' he said. 'And the boat I'm on crosses the Channel several times a year. I'm prepared to risk my life to smuggle Tyndale's translation into England. What have I got to lose? If I die, I go to heaven.'

The next time the young man's boat docked in Antwerp, where Tyndale then lived, a shadowy figure approached him one night, carrying a large package under his cloak. A password was exchanged, and, without another word, the figure followed the sailor on to the boat and down into the hold. It was the middle of the night, and nearly everyone else was asleep, exhausted after their voyage. Only whispers were spoken, but enough was said for the young man to be sure that this was no mere messenger with English Bibles; this was William Tyndale himself. He wasn't content to translate God's Word; he wanted to do all he could to get it to England.

When the package was safely stowed, the two men slunk off the ship. Before they parted, Tyndale put both hands on the young man's shoulders and prayed for his safety and the safe passage of the precious parcel.

As he fell asleep that night, William thought of his trip to the ship, and he broke into a wide smile. 'The Word of God in our own language! I remember mother speaking to me in the kitchen ... she never understood a word of Latin. Now women like her will be able to hear God's Word in their own tongue! Perhaps they'll be able to tell their children about it ... even when they are churning the butter.'

'Thank you for seeing me,' Henry Phillips said, when he first met Tyndale in 1535. 'It's taken me a long time to meet you face to face.'

'I have to be careful,' William explained. 'There are those who would rather see me dead than alive.'

Phillips pretended that the very thought shocked him.

'What is it I can do for you?' asked Tyndale.

His visitor poured out a lying story, saying that he was a Christian in need of help. But he was a spy, and a cunning one. Tyndale fell into the trap that was laid for him. He was arrested and put into prison where he was kept for over a year.

From his prison cell, Tyndale wrote to the governor asking for some of his possessions to be brought to him. The weather was cold, and he asked for his warm coat and cap and a woollen shirt. But most of all what he wanted were candles and his Hebrew Bible, grammar and dictionary so that he could continue his work of translation.

Eventually he was tried and found guilty of being a heretic, someone who spoke against what the Roman Church taught. For weeks after that the prison and Church authorities tried to make William change his beliefs and accept what the Church taught. But they failed miserably.

In October 1536 Tyndale was taken from his cell and strangled. His body was not buried; it was publicly burned.

Just before he died, William Tyndale prayed, 'Lord, open the King of England's eyes.'

He didn't live to see it, but God answered his prayer. Soon after his death, a copy of the Bible in English was placed in every Church in England by order of the King, and ordinary people were encouraged to read it for themselves.

FACT FILE

Printing: This is a method of producing many copies of a document by pressing an inked pattern into fabric or metal. The oldest method of printing is letterpress. This method was used in Japan before A.D. 770. The unusual thing about letterpress printing is that the metal letters have to be arranged in a tray backwards, reading right to left instead of left to right. This is so that when the page is printed, the letters will read the correct way on the paper. The first person in Europe to use this type of printing successfully was Johan Gutenberg in about 1438.

Keynote: As a young man, William Tyndale wanted to know why the Bible was not in English. There are many people groups that still do not have God's Word in their own language. Wycliffe Bible Translators work very hard to translate the Bible into the language of every tribe and nation.

William Tyndale

Think: Many people risked their lives so that the Bible would be available in a language that ordinary people understood. They risked their lives to print and distribute God's Word. In some countries Christians still risk their lives to get God's Word to their friends and neighbours. Is God's Word precious to you? Would you risk your life to read it? Would you do anything so that your friends and family could read it for themselves?

Prayer: Lord God, help me to understand and treasure your word, the Bible. Forgive me for disobeying what you say in it. Thank you for all those people who teach and explain it to me. Be with them and encourage them. Amen.

Hugh Latimer

Hugh felt as though he was on top of the world. 'Are you all right?' his father asked. His smile told the answer. 'I'll make a king's horseman of you yet,' he said to his son. Hugh sat as tall as he could, held his head high and nudged the horse to move quicker.

'Not too fast,' came the warning. 'Remember she's not been ridden often and she's not used to you at all.'

'One day I'll ride for the King,' Hugh exclaimed. 'By then she'll go like the wind.'

'Not if you fall from a frisky mount and knock your head off,' his dad laughed. 'Take her out every day for a short time, and she'll calm down soon.'

'Once round the meadow?' Hugh wheedled.

Mr Latimer looked at the pony; she seemed calm enough. 'Once, and take her slowly.'

Hugh pretended he was a soldier riding behind the King. With a straight back and head high, he walked the pony round the meadow. 'He holds himself well,' his father thought as he watched.

'That's enough for today,' Mr Latimer announced, when the eight-year-old pulled the pony to a stop at his side. 'Now give her a treat and leave her to rest.'

Hugh pulled some handfuls of long grass from the side of the ploughed field and fed them to the pony then led her home. 'I think you should go and give your mother a hand with the milking,' the man said. 'If you ask her to fill the wooden buckets only half-full you'll be able to carry them for her. And there might be a white moustache for you at the end of the job.'

The boy grinned. There was nothing he enjoyed better than a cup of warm, frothy milk straight from the cow, and his father often teased him because the froth usually left him with a white, milky moustache.

'I'm glad you've come,' said Mrs Latimer, 'because I've a lot to do before the sun goes down.'

'Dad said I could help carry the milk.'

'And so you can, but the milk I'd like you to carry is a half-bucketful to poor Mrs Fletcher. Her children have whooping cough and they need all the good food they can get. She's a poor widow woman and can't afford to buy extra milk for the boys.'

'It's a long way to Mrs Fletcher's,' Hugh said, looking at the size of the bucket.

'So it is, but I'll make it easier for you by giving you some butter and cheese as well, and a small cabbage from the garden.'

Hugh thought his mum was joking. 'That'll make it a lot easier!' he laughed.

But it did. Mrs Latimer hung the bucket of milk from one end of a short pole. Then she wrapped the cheese, butter and cabbage in a cloth and hung them from the other end.

'Now,' she said, 'you'll discover how easy it can be to carry things.' She hoisted the pole on to Hugh's shoulders. 'Just keep your head held high and you'll hardly feel the weight.'

To his surprise he found out that was true. 'I thought this looked hard when I saw my sisters doing it,' he said to himself, as he reached Mrs Fletcher's, 'but it's not.'

'I'm home!' Hugh shouted, as he neared his father's small farm. 'Watch out!' a voice replied, and he ducked. Without thinking he'd come out of a clump of trees just where his brothers were practising archery. Hugh ducked behind a tree until a voice told him it was safe to come out.

'Your turn,' his brother said. 'If you're big enough to carry loads, you're big enough for this bow.' Hugh looked at his brother's bow.

It seemed huge compared to his own one. 'Stand straight,' the older boy said. 'That's right; your back should be as straight as a soldier's. Now hold your bow firmly. Head up! You need to keep your neck straight and your head high.' Concentrating hard, Hugh pulled the arrow back and held it till his brother told him to shoot. 'Now!' A final pull, then the arrow shot off and headed straight for the target. 'Well done!' his brother laughed. 'You'll make an archer one day.' Hugh grinned. 'The best one in Thurcastone.' 'Maybe the best in England,' added the older boy. 'Maybe.'

'Hugh tries very hard,' Mr Latimer told his wife one day, as they worked together thinning turnips. She straightened her aching back. 'He's not strong,' she said, 'but he's got a good head on his shoulders. He's smart.'

'I think he should go to the university when he finishes school. He'll never be able to work the farm for a living.'

'That would cost a lot of money,' commented Mrs Latimer.

Her husband stood up and stretched. 'We're not rich,' he said, 'but we're not poor either. And if he does well enough, he'd be able to make his own way in the world.'

'I knew he could do it,' boasted proud Mr Latimer some years later when, in 1510, Hugh was paid to work for Cambridge University. 'He studied so hard and did so well that they're willing to pay him.'

'The people in the village thought sending him to university was a waste of money. This will show them they were wrong!' his wife laughed. 'I always knew he was gifted.'

Two years later their youngest son became a preacher and a very eager one.

'What do you think of this new teaching?' a friend asked Hugh. 'There are some who say that the Pope isn't head of the Church.'

'So I've heard. But they'll come to a bad end if they teach that kind of nonsense. Of course the Pope is head of the Church.'

'They say that's not in the Bible,' went on his friend.

'But it's what the Church teaches,' Hugh said. 'And that's just as important as the Bible.'

'There's more and more of that kind of teaching around,' concluded his companion.

Latimer scowled, then said, 'I'll do my very best to stamp out such rubbish!' For some time that's exactly what he did.

'May I make my confession to you?' Thomas Bilney asked Latimer.

'Of course, come to my study,' the priest said. But Bilney believed in the truth of the Bible, and rather than make a confession, he told Hugh what he believed. Latimer listened, because that was what a priest had to do, but soon he was listening because he really wanted to hear what the man was saying. 'Could this be true?' he wondered. That day was the beginning of a great change in Hugh's life. Very soon afterwards he trusted in the Lord Jesus as his Saviour.

'You're going to have to be careful,' one of the university staff warned him. 'You're getting a reputation as a Reformer. Surely you don't believe all that rubbish.'

Latimer smiled sadly at the man. 'Not long ago I thought it was rubbish. Now I know it's the best news in the whole world.'

'What do you mean?' spat out the reply.

Hugh took his colleague by the arm. 'Let's go for a walk and a talk.'

As they strolled along the banks of the River Cam, the new Christian explained what had happened to him.

'What I do is this,' Latimer explained. 'I look at what the Bible teaches and what the Church teaches and, where the two are not the same, I know I should believe the Bible.'

'Why?'

'Because it's God's Word, and he doesn't tell lies.'

'But isn't what the Church says important too?'

'Yes,' Hugh agreed. 'But the Church can be mistaken. God never makes mistakes.'

They walked in silence for a while, as the man thought about what had been said.

'So what does the Church teach that isn't in the Bible?' Latimer's friend asked eventually.

'For one thing it teaches that the Pope is head of the Church where the Bible says that Christ is head.'

'Rubbish!' announced the other man.

'For another, the Church teaches that every time the Mass is held, Jesus is sacrificed again. But the Bible says he was sacrificed once and for all on the cross.'

His companion stopped walking, turned to Hugh Latimer and, with his face red with rage, said, 'You should be burned for saying these things! And from now on you're no friend of mine.' He strode off in the direction of Cambridge.

'What we need,' Hugh said to some men who thought as he did, 'is the Bible in English. People could then read it for themselves.'

'Watch where you say that,' one of them warned Latimer. 'It could get you into trouble.'

And it did.

'What a stupid idea!' a monk said, when he heard the idea. 'Imagine what would happen if common people had the Bible in English. Jesus said that a little yeast makes bread rise and he compared it to what a little sin does in a life. If ordinary folk read what Jesus said, they'd stop putting yeast in bread, and we'd all be eating hard biscuits! Giving men the Bible in English is the stupidest suggestion I've heard in years! In any case, if you did that, they would stop listening to what the priests say.'

'That might be good,' thought Latimer.

Although Hugh was not popular with everyone, some still realised that he was a good priest. Because of them he was made Bishop of Worcester. But he felt he had to resign when the King refused to allow the Roman Church in England to change into a Church that believed and taught the Bible. Many people loved Hugh's preaching, but the bishops and priests did not.

'The time has come to resign,' he told a group of friends who met in his room. 'And that's what I'm going to do.' Hugh took off his bishop's clothes then suddenly did a little skip in the middle of his room. 'That feels better!' he laughed. 'That feels much better!'

'I've come with news for you,' a messenger told Latimer. 'You've to go to London to stand trial for heresy.'

'That's not news to me,' Hugh said. 'I've been expecting it.'

The trial was much as he thought it would be, and he was thrown into the Tower of London.

'That was terrible,' complained one of his friends. 'The court made him out to be a fool.'

'And a heretic.'

'And a traitor to the crown!' added another.

'But did you see Hugh during the trial?' someone asked. 'All the time they were insulting him, he held his head high.'

'I wonder if he'll ever be free again,' one of his friends said sadly.

'At least he has the company of Master Ridley and Dr Cranmer,' the oldest man said. 'But with all three of these fine Reformers in prison, we'll have to work extra hard to preach about Jesus.'

'You're going to Oxford,' barked the prison guard to each of the three men who had been held in separate cells.

'Why?' Ridley asked.

'You'll stand trial there,' he was told. 'And if justice is done, you'll be put to death for the lies you've been telling.'

On 28th September, 1555, their trial began.

'The charge is that you are teaching lies about the Mass,' the Officer of the Court announced. 'Do you deny the charges?'

The men admitted their teaching. 'Will you publicly deny the truth of what you've been preaching?' they were asked.

With his head held high, Latimer said he would not.

'You're an old man,' one of those in court told Hugh. 'For goodness' sake and for the sake of your poor old body just agree with them.'

Hugh shook his head and held it high. 'No,' he said clearly and firmly.

The next day they were asked the same question again. 'No,' the men said. 'We cannot deny the truth of the Bible.'

When they were taken back to their cells, Latimer prayed three things: that God would help him to stand up for the truth till he died; that the Lord would have the gospel of Jesus preached throughout England; and that Elizabeth would become queen and be blessed.

'Guilty!' the Officer of the Court shouted. 'This court finds them guilty!' Then turning to the prisoners, he said, 'You will be burned at the stake for your lies.' A terrible sermon was preached to them, but they held their heads high till it was over.

'Will you deny your teaching?' Latimer and Ridley were asked one last time as they were taken out to be killed.

'I will never deny it,' said both men. The two Reformers were stripped, apart from burial gowns. They gave away all they had with them then walked calmly to the stake.

'Together!' was the command.

Hugh was chained to one side of the stake, his friend to the other. A bag of gunpowder was hung round their necks and the fire lit.

Hugh held his head high and prayed, 'O Father in heaven, receive my soul.'

'Lord have mercy on me,' prayed Ridley.

The fire raged; the gunpowder exploded, and two brave men went to heaven. But their prayers for England were answered, and a Church grew up which began to teach the Bible.

FACT FILE
Tower of London: The Tower of London is beside the River Thames on the east side of London. It has been a palace, a fortress and a prison. Many famous people - queens, dukes and churchmen - have been executed, murdered or imprisoned within its walls. Prisoners are no longer kept in the Tower, and today it is an ancient monument and tourist attraction. As well as being used to house the crown jewels, it is home to a large colony of ravens.

Keynote: Hugh Latimer believed that Jesus Christ was the head of the Church and not the Pope. Jesus died so that those who believe in his name can have eternal life. No one else has ever or will ever do that. Those who believe in the name of Jesus Christ are the Church. Jesus, their Lord and Master, is the Church's leader and head.

Think: Latimer and Ridley both said that they could not deny the truth of the Bible. Think about the Bible for a moment. Who wrote it? Though prophets, disciples and men of God did the actual physical writing, it was God who inspired all the words. God was the one behind it all. Why does that make the Bible special and unique? It is because the Bible is true from beginning to end. God is truth and he cannot tell lies. God wants to bring people to himself. He wants and longs to save you.

Prayer: Lord Jesus, it is sad to think of the violence and hatred that people show to each other. In the past Christians have suffered and died because they believed in you. And that is still happening in some lands today. You suffered, too, so that we can have eternal life. We don't deserve this but we thank you for all that you have done. Amen.

John Calvin

John sat on his mother's bed. She was unwell and found his games tiring, but she enjoyed it when they sat and talked together.

'Tell me about when you were a little girl,' he said.

His mother smiled. 'My father and mother live in a small town right in the north of France. They have an inn, and when I was a girl, people were always coming and going. Sometimes I hid in the kitchen and listened to what the grown-ups were talking about. Most of them were traders on their way to sell things in England.'

'Is my father a trader?' the five-year-old asked.

Smiling at the thought, his mother explained, 'No, he is a lawyer and he works at the Cathedral here in Noyon.'

'What do lawyers do?'

'All sorts of things,' she said. 'Sometimes his work is about buying and selling land.'

'So he is a trader.'

'I suppose in a way he is,' laughed his mother. 'But it's not his own things that he's buying and selling; everything he works with belongs to the Church.'

'The Church must be very rich,' the little boy thought aloud.

'Yes,' agreed his mother. 'I think it is.'

'Shh! Please be quiet,' the woman told John, just a few months later. 'It's not nice to make a noise in a house of the dead.'

'But I want my mother!' he sobbed. 'I don't want her to be dead.'

'Well, you'll just have to get used to it. And you'll have to be quiet too. Your poor father needs peace.'

The child didn't know what peace was, but he knew there was something that he needed to help his sore heart.

'Do I need peace?' he asked the woman who had come to prepare his mother's body for the funeral.

When she looked at him crossly, he went outside to get away from her.

From that day on, life was different for young John Calvin. He did all the things that had to be done, but nothing was ever the same. There was no mother to answer his questions or to kiss him better when he fell and grazed his knees. He must have missed her softness, her night-time kisses and their special times together. Life must have had its sad times for little John Calvin.

'I have something I want to explain to you,' his father told John some seven years later, in 1521. 'An arrangement has been made to give you a job.'

John's face fell. 'But I don't want a job. I want to study.'

His father sat down. 'If you would just listen to what I'm trying to say!'

Calvin took a seat in front of his father. 'This is something that happens in the Church. You are given a job and are paid for it, but you don't actually have to do the work.'

'Why?'

'Because someone else does it for you.'

'So what's the job and why doesn't the other person get the pay?'

'The job is looking after a church, and he does get paid, though not very much. That leaves plenty for you.'

'What do I need the money for?' John asked puzzled.

'Education doesn't come cheap,' his father said. 'The money will help pay for it.'

John puzzled over that. It seemed to him a very odd thing but he was glad to have the money.

When he was fourteen years old, Calvin went off to university, first in Paris where he studied theology (that's the study of God), then, because his father wanted him to, he studied law in another French university. But before he had finished his studies in law, John's father died. He was on his own and could make his own decisions.

'I've decided to go back to Paris to study Greek and Hebrew,' he told a friend.

'That's a dangerous thing to do,' the other young man laughed. 'If you read the Bible, you might become like that man Luther!'

Calvin looked his friend in the eye. 'I don't think I'm as easily convinced as he was,' he announced. 'I was brought up in the Church. It pays for my education. If you think I'm likely to leave it after all that and to start preaching that it's not telling the truth, you can think again.'

'Keep your head on!' said his friend. 'I was only joking!'

Within a very short time, John Calvin had done exactly what his friend had joked about. 'I was absolutely caught up in all the superstitions of the Church,' he wrote later, 'then I was suddenly converted, and God tamed my heart and made me teachable.' When he wrote to his friend to tell him what had happened, the letter that came back was not very encouraging.

'You've made a brave decision,' it read, 'but a very dangerous one. If I were you, I'd prepare to leave Paris, because if you don't go, you'll be chased out. The Church and the King don't like Reformers. Are you quite sure you really are one of them?'

'I'm certain,' Calvin wrote back. 'The Church is full of things that need reform. Think about it. My education was paid for by money the Church gave me to do nothing! And some poor soul did the work and got virtually nothing for it – all because my father was a cathedral lawyer! That can't be right. It's one of many ways in which the Church is wrong. You were right about being chased out of Paris … this letter is from Geneva which I think will now be my home.'

'What will you do now?' he was asked by a Swiss Christian he met at church.

'The thing I'm best at is studying, so I think that's what I should continue to do,' replied John. 'It's all very well leaving the Roman Church because of all the wrongs in it, but the Reformed Church will also make serious mistakes unless we really know what the Bible says and stick to it. I think that's what God is calling me to do.'

'It's a huge job,' his new friend said, smiling. 'But God only gives work like that to those who can do it.'

'I feel safe here,' John told a Genevan friend in August 1536.

'I know what you mean. It's great that the people here voted to live according to the Bible and to abolish the teaching of the Roman Church in the city.'

'It means I can relax for a while and get on with my writing without worrying about spies tracking me down.'

'I hope you'll be here for more than a while,' another Reformer said. 'We need you to help establish a church in Geneva.'

But two years later Calvin was on the move again. The town council had changed, and he was no longer welcome. 'Moving won't stop my work,' he told his Swiss friends, as he packed up his papers. 'A student can study anywhere.'

'I have never been so happy in all my life,' John said. 'This year in Strasbourg has been wonderful.'

'In what way?' Idelette asked.

'Because,' he smiled, 'you agreed to marry me and you've given me an instant family of children.'

Idelette looked serious, but just for a moment. 'When my husband was dying, it worried him what would happen to the children and to me. I never dreamed that I would love again and that my children would have such a fine stepfather. It's been a very happy year for me too.'

'The only thing is that I don't get the same peace to write,' John said, half seriously.

'You knew what you were taking on!' his wife laughed. 'And you're not doing too badly. You've just finished a book and you're working on another one already.'

'I think the time has come to go back to Geneva,' John told his wife in 1541. 'I've worked out a system of church government that I think the Genevans will approve of.'

They did, even if they didn't carry it out quite as Calvin would have liked.

Reformers came from all over Europe to study with Calvin, many of them former priests in the Roman Church. Their discussions went on for hours and hours.

'I'd like to give you a subject,' a Frenchman said at a meeting one day.

'What is it?' asked Calvin. 'I'll speak on it if I can.'

'Please explain predestination,' the man begged. 'I find it so confusing.'

Calvin stood up, rubbed his chin and began. 'The Bible teaches that before creation God in his great love chose some people to be his own. During their time on earth these people will trust in Jesus and when they die they will go to be with him.

What the Bible teaches is good news – that all those who trust in Jesus will go to heaven. Is that good news?' he asked the Frenchman.

'Yes,' was the reply.

'And that,' his teacher concluded, 'is predestination.'

'My heart is broken,' John Calvin said when, in 1549, Idelette died. 'First, my only son dies as a child, then my wife after just eleven years of marriage.'

'But you have us,' his stepson told him. 'We're your family.'

Calvin put his hand on the young man's shoulder. 'I know,' he said. 'And it's very hard for you all to lose your father, then your mother, when you're still so young.'

'But we're not alone,' the boy said. 'You have us and we have you.'

The man looked up into the strong, young face. 'You're right,' he agreed. 'And God will care for us.'

Some years later a discussion was held about a plan Calvin had for the city.

'It's a very interesting idea,' the Council decided.

'It would be good if Geneva had its own Academy. People would come from all over Europe to study here,' one man said.

'Yes, and that would bring money to the city,' another commented.

'And trade,' added a third.

'Do we agree to go ahead?' the chairman asked, when it came time to vote.

Calvin was very pleased with the result. The Council voted yes. 'I hope it will become the centre of reformed thinking in Europe,' John told his congregation. 'All roads will lead to Geneva.'

'Good morning, gentlemen,' John Calvin said to a class at the Academy in the early 1560s. 'Before we begin, I would like to know where you all come from.'

'I'm German,' one said.

'France,' another called out.

'My home is in Scotland.'

'I'm English,' a voice came from the back of the room.

'Is everyone else Swiss?' questioned Calvin.

'I've come from the Netherlands,' a deep voice said.

'This class is a vision come true,' John told his students. 'You have come from all over Europe, and when you leave, you'll take the Word of God back home with you.'

'It's great to study with you, Mr Calvin,' a former priest told his teacher. 'And all your many books are brilliant. I know I can believe every word you say.'

'That, young man,' John told him, 'is probably the most frightening thing anyone has ever said to me.' His pupil looked shocked. 'You came out of the Roman Church because it was teaching you things that were untrue, and now you're prepared to believe all I say. For goodness' sake use the brain God has given you. I will never deliberately misguide you, but you must check everything I say, everything anyone says, by what is written in the Bible. That is the only source of truth.'

The young man was upset, and Calvin felt suddenly sorry for him. 'Listen to me,' he said. 'I'm just an ordinary human being like yourself, and I, too, can make mistakes. If you ever find yourself thinking that I'm special, ask someone who knows me well. If I have a pain, I'm like a bear with a sore head. And if I go to bed with a stomach ache, I assume I'll die before morning, but I've not done that yet.'

'I really am not well,' John told a fellow teacher. 'I'm not sure that I'll manage to lecture today.' A buzz went round the Academy. 'Was John Calvin ill? Or was this just another of his days of thinking he was worse than he really was. 'He isn't actually looking very good,' one of his students commented. 'And his colour's a bit odd,' added another. They were right. John Calvin was ill and he never got better. Having influenced the Reformation in Europe more than any other man, he died on 27th May, 1564.

FACT FILE
Geneva: This city is now part of the country of Switzerland and has been since 1815. Before that it was French, and prior to 1798 Geneva was an independent city. The International Red Cross was founded in Geneva in 1863 by Henri Dunant, and after World War I the city was chosen for the headquarters of the League of Nations. It is well known for the production of watches, jewellery and chocolate.

Keynote: John Calvin knew that he had good points and bad points and that in the end people shouldn't just accept everything he said as true. Everyone can make mistakes and we all do. It is up to you to make sure that you study the Bible for yourself. Then when you hear someone teaching about the Bible, you will, with God's help, know if they are speaking the truth or not.

Think: 'Take the word of God home with you.' This is an important thing to do. John's students took God's Word home with them from Geneva. You can bring God's Word back to your family if you go to church or Sunday school. You can bring it back to your school. Think about ways you can do this. Perhaps you could start a Christian club at school? Perhaps you could ask your parents to read the Bible with you every morning? How about asking your best friend to come to Christian camp with you next summer?

 Prayer: Thank you God that you never lie. You are always truthful. You are truth. Help me to read your Word, the Bible, and know the truth for myself. Even little children can understand your truth and follow you. Amen.

John Knox

John pulled up his sleeves and lay down on the rocks beside the River Tyne near his home in the small Scottish village of Haddington. He chose the place carefully so that his shadow didn't fall on the water. Because he knew the river well, he knew that under the rocky outcrop on which he was lying there was still water where fish rested as they swam up and down river.

Slowly he slid his hand into the water, so slowly that there wasn't a hint of a splash or ripple. Then he lay absolutely still for several minutes. 'Gently does it,' he thought, as he lowered his hand just a tiny bit and waited yet again. It must have taken him several minutes to get it up to the elbow, but he knew it was worth being patient. One false move and that would be the end of his guddling for fish for the day. Because he had studied the layout of the rocks, he knew exactly where the fish lay.

For minutes he stayed completely still, letting any fish looking in the direction of his hand lose interest in it and settle back down again. 'Go for it!' he said to himself. He made a grab for a cleft in the rock and caught a slithering, swishing, fighting fish in his hand. He scuttled to his feet and looked at his catch. 'Not bad,' he said aloud. 'Not bad at all.'

Leaving the River Tyne behind, John went back to the trees where he'd agreed to meet his friends. They were also guddling for fish, but they spread themselves out along the river, or each would disturb the others.

'Did you catch any?' asked the boy who was already there.

John held up his fish by the tail. 'And here comes Angus,' he added, pointing to a third boy who was waving a fish in the air. 'Let's get the fire going.'

John collected dry gorse, small twigs and some bigger branches as well. With a little bit of effort the gorse was soon sparking into life, and the three boys sat down to wait for their fire to blaze and begin to die down before they cooked their lunch. When all that was left was the glowing embers, they laid their fish on the fire and covered them with the hot red branches.

'Smells good,' said John. 'And I'm starving.'

They chatted until they thought their fish were ready then, using thin green branches they knew would not go on fire, they brushed the embers off their fish and pulled their dinners from the fire. 'Delicious!' Angus said. John licked his lips and wiped them with his sleeve. 'Guddled fish roasted outside on a fire is the best meal in the world.'

'Time to be going,' one of the boys said, when all that was left were three fish skeletons.

'But let's do this again soon.'

John knelt by the ashes and began to clear them up. Thinking they would be cold, he lifted up a handful to scatter.

'Ouch!' he yelled. 'I've burnt myself!'

Although he was brave, he was very near to tears.

'Let me see,' demanded Angus. By the time John had dusted away the ashes, his hand was very red. 'It's so sore,' he said through his tears. 'I've burnt it badly.'

Go and stick your hand in the river,' Angus suggested. 'That'll cool it down.'

By the time John Knox reached the river, he could hardly see through his tears. The cold water did help, but his hand was very painful for several days, especially in the evenings when his mother lit the fire, and the heat made it even sorer.

'Can we go and have a last guddle for fish?' John suggested to his companions a few summers later. 'It's the last chance we'll have before I go away to St Andrews University.'

'On one condition,' Angus said. 'That you don't decide to cook your hand as well as your fish!'

John laughed. 'No way! When I was a boy, I used to wonder how hot fire was and I discovered the answer that day.'

That conversation came into Knox's mind as soon as he arrived in St Andrews, because right in front of the university was an area of scorched earth.

'That's where Patrick Hamilton was burned at the stake,' he was told. John shuddered at the thought of the pain the man suffered.

'I've heard about that,' he said to his fellow student, 'but seeing where it happened makes me feel sick.'

'All he'd done was preach the Bible,' the other young man commented.

'Not the way the Roman Church likes it preached,' concluded Knox.

After leaving university, John was ordained as a priest and, among other things, he worked as a chaplain to some wealthy families, and tutor to their sons. Nothing much is known about that part of his life, but by the time he comes into the Church's story again, he was a Christian and preaching the gospel fearlessly.

'Will you come with me to hear George Wishart?' a friend asked him in 1545.

'Yes,' Knox said. 'I've heard about him and I'd like to hear what he has to say for himself.'

As they travelled, the two men talked.

'This is a terrible time to live but an exciting one too,' Knox said. 'The Roman Church is in such a mess, and it's not helped here in Scotland by the Queen being a believer in the Roman ways.'

'One day we may even have to leave the Church and follow the European Reformers. They're teaching the Bible while the Church is just preaching traditions. Maybe George Wishart is the man who will lead Scotland through her own reformation.'

When John Knox heard Wishart preach, he was so thrilled that he spent three months going round the country with him telling people to believe in the Lord rather than in the Church. But the following spring Wishart was arrested. John was with him till midnight on the night before he was to be martyred. The thought of his friend being burned at the stake appalled Knox.

'Go home to your family and God bless you,' Wishart told him, as night became morning. 'It's enough that one dies.'

John left and heard later that day that George Wishart had been strangled and his body burned.

'People all know you now,' John's friend said. 'And they're out to get you. The Romanists in Scotland won't stop until you're out of the way.'

'He was right,' Knox often thought over the next nineteen months. 'It was only weeks after he warned me I wasn't safe in Scotland that I was captured, and I've been a slave on this galley ever since. I wonder if I'll ever be free again to preach Jesus to my own Scottish folk.'

A whip hit his shoulder. 'Pull man! Pull your weight!' Taking the oar more firmly in his aching hands, he pulled it towards himself, then pushed it away.

'Pull! Pull! Pull!' the man shouted, until Knox's oar was in time with the others.

As he rowed with every ounce of his strength, he remembered back to his boyhood. 'How I loved the River Tyne,' he thought. 'Now I think I'd rather not see water ever again!'

'Pull!' a voice roared in his ear as the whip hit his shoulder yet again.

'Is that really John?' someone asked, after Knox was released to England. 'He seems so much older and thinner than I remember him.'

'That's what a year and a half as a galley slave did to him,' his companion explained. 'Another few months and I think he'd have died. But we need him alive and well because we need his preaching.'

Knox's freedom to preach only lasted until 1553 when he had to flee for his life. He eventually reached Geneva and met and studied with John Calvin.

'We need you in Scotland,' the messenger said. 'I've been sent to take you back.'

'Is it any safer now,' Knox asked, 'than when I had to leave?'

'Probably not, but we need you.'

John asked the man why he should go.

'The new, young Queen Mary is on the throne. She's a Romanist, and if you don't come back and help us, there's a chance that Scotland will become as Romanist as she is. She's just a young woman,' the messenger concluded, 'and perhaps you'll be able to influence her to believe in the true religion.'

'Perhaps,' said John. 'It seems that I should go back. I've learned such a lot from

Calvin, and the time has come to pass it on to the Church in Scotland.'

On 4th May, 1559, when Knox preached his first sermon back in Edinburgh, it was not to a Church congregation but to an army. The Protestants (those who protested against Romanist teaching) had gathered as an army for fear of a war. Mary, Queen of Scots' husband was on the French throne, and together they had gathered troops against the Protestants. There was a possibility that the young reformed Church could be wiped out. But that was not what happened. England sent troops north, the French troops left and it looked as though things were going well.

'What do you see as the way ahead?' Knox and the reformers were often asked, even by the Scottish Parliament.

Having written a book on the subject, it was John who explained the plan. 'We will worship simply without any of the rituals of the Roman Church. We'll have no idols and no suggestion that the bread and wine are the Lord's actual body and blood. We'll have no bishops ruling over us, and no Pope as the head of the church. Instead, elders will be elected and they'll only serve for one year at a time. They'll help the ministers. And ministers will be elected too, not given jobs by bishops.'

'It was a disgrace before,' one of his friends said. 'Bishops made men ministers because they owed them a favour, not because they were Christians. And if they owed them several favours, they gave them a number of churches. They got the pay for each of them and often did no work at all! Not only that; sometimes they gave their friends' children jobs as priests when they were just eleven or twelve years old!'

'And there should be a church and a school in every parish,' Knox continued, when his friend had finished speaking.

'That's a great idea,' he was told. 'But how will it be paid for?'

'The Church owns hundreds of miles of Scotland. That will be sold to raise the money.'

'How dare that man make decisions for Scotland!' Mary, Queen of Scots fumed. 'I'm on the throne, not him!'

'And how dare you tell me what to do with my life!' she roared on one of the times they met. Mary was so angry that she wept with rage as he left.

'You've gone too far this time,' the Queen told him when, in 1563, he preached against the Mass. 'You've gone one step too far!' She didn't stop from that day until she had him arrested for treason.

'That's the end of him!' Mary announced. 'He'll not bother me again!'

But Knox was set free, and Mary had no peace from the man who wanted Scotland reformed, until four years later when she left the throne to her young son, James.

'Are you comfortable? Do you want me to read to you?' Mrs Knox asked her husband in 1572. He was in bed having suffered from a stroke.

'Yes,' he said. 'I'm comfortable. And I'm just content to think,' he replied. 'You could maybe read to me later.'

'What are you thinking?'

John lay back on his pillows. 'I'm thinking of Scotland,' he said, 'and of the troubled times she's been through. When I started off as a priest in the Roman Church, I never dreamed I'd spend most of my life telling people that much of what the Church taught was wrong and they should look away from the Church to Jesus. I just hope and pray that the new Church, the Church of Scotland, will always preach Jesus, that it won't forget its message.'

'It cost you and the other reformers such a lot to bring reformation to Scotland,' Mrs Knox said. 'All those months on the galley were terrible for you.'

'They were,' he admitted. 'But I'm dying in my bed. Think of Patrick Hamilton being burned at the stake and what it cost him. And my dear George Wishart; think of him being strangled before his body was burned. It didn't cost me as much as it cost them.'

There was a long silence. 'Is he sleeping?' Mrs Knox wondered. John was not.

'You could read to me now,' he said weakly, 'from 1 Corinthians 15 and John 17.'

With tears in her eyes, his wife read, 'Death has been swallowed up in victory. Where, O death, is your victory? Where, O death, is your sting?'

Then from John's Gospel she read Christ's prayer, 'Father, I want those you have given me to be with me where I am, and to see my glory, the glory you have given me because you loved me before the creation of the world.'

That chapter was the last John Knox was to hear on earth. Just a short while later he was with Jesus in glory.

FACT FILE

Mary, Queen of Scots: She was born in 1542, and her father died just after her birth. As a result, she was crowned Queen of Scotland as a young baby. At the age of five she was engaged to be married to the heir to the French throne. However, two years after their marriage in 1558, Mary's husband died, and she returned to Scotland. She married again, but in 1567 her second husband was murdered. Many suspected her of planning the murder so she was imprisoned and forced to give up her crown to her young son James VI. She was finally executed by the orders of the English Queen, Elizabeth I, at Fotheringay Castle on 8th February, 1587.

Keynote: John asked his wife to read the Bible to him before he died. The words were, 'Death has been swallowed up in victory.' This means that because Jesus died for our sins on the cross - and rose back to life again - death has been defeated. Although

Christians die, their souls have eternal life in heaven where death can never touch them again.

Think: John Knox realised that following Christ had not cost him as much as Patrick Hamilton or George Wishart. It cost them their lives. What did it cost John? It meant hardship and a struggle. Do you follow Christ? What does it cost you? Jesus told his followers to take up their cross and to follow him. That means to obey God's Word and stand up for the truth. Don't look back. Don't give up.

Prayer: Lord Jesus, thank you for defeating death. When we think of what it cost you, it is amazing. You suffered like no one else when you took the punishment for our sins. But you rose again, and your power broke the power of sin and death. Help me to believe in you and your power. Give me a knowledge of my sin and of your goodness. Amen.

Lord Shaftesbury

Little Anthony Ashley shivered as he heard his father rage at his three older sisters. 'Had they made a noise?' he wondered. 'Or had they said something without being asked?' There seemed to be so many things that made their father rage, and all of them made six-year-old Anthony shiver. Even his tummy shivered inside himself, and from time to time when that happened, he was sick and got a telling-off for that.

Something touched his arm, and he jumped. His feet actually left the floor. 'It's all right,' a soft voice said. 'Come into the nursery away from the noise.' The child began to relax as Maria soothed him with soft words. But when the nursery door closed behind them, his little legs buckled, and he fell to the floor sobbing. Maria, whose job it was to look after the four Ashley children, sat down and gently lifted the boy on to her knee.

'Why are we all so sad?' Anthony asked, when he looked up at Maria and saw tears in her eyes.

'Your papa and mama are very important people,' she explained, 'and it's just when they are interrupted that they get cross with you.'

He looked at her and knew that she was telling him the truth. But he knew, too, that there were so many important things going on in his parents' lives that he was always an interruption.

'I want to run away,' he said, blowing his nose hard. 'Are you sleeping?' Anthony asked, when he saw Maria's closed eyes.

'No, Master Anthony,' she said. 'I'm praying.'

'Will you pray for me?' he pleaded.

She hugged him close. 'I pray for you all every day, over and over again.'

'Does God hear you?' he questioned.

Maria stood him up in front of her, all the better to look right into his eyes. 'Master Anthony,' she said in a soft but serious voice, 'God hears every word. He hears every telling-off you get and sees every tear you shed. And when you want to run away, there is only one place to which it's safe to run.'

Catching something of the seriousness of the maid's tone, he listened very carefully. 'Where is that?' he asked.

'The only safe place to be is in the arms of Jesus,' she explained.

Anthony looked sad. 'But I can only go there when I die, and that may be a long time away.'

Pulling him back on to her knee and giving him a warm hug, Maria explained that if he puts his trust in the Lord Jesus, the Saviour would keep him safe in his arms through all the hard things he would meet in life.

There was no time Anthony Ashley needed to hear that more than when, just a year or two later, he was sent away to school. Knowing that tears would bring a raging from his father, Anthony just shook hands with his much-loved Maria as he left. That's what his father saw. What he did not see were the tears and the hugs and the prayers the two had had together as Maria dressed the young scholar in his new school clothes. There were no tears when he left for school because, apart from missing Maria and his sisters, he was not sorry to leave home.

'Carry this for me, brat!' an older boy ordered, as soon as he clapped eyes on the new pupil. Anthony looked puzzled. Was he speaking to him? A punch on the cheek made it clear that he was. But before he could pick up the boy's books, he was jumped on by two others who, along with the first thug, gave him a beating much like his father's. As suddenly as it had begun, the assault stopped. 'Get up,' a master roared. The three scrambled to their feet, knowing that if they didn't move quickly, they'd get the master's boot in their sides. But Anthony, not realising that some of his new teachers were as cruel as the children, didn't move fast enough to avoid a nasty and quite deliberate kick. 'Get on your way,' the man growled.

Things went from bad to worse, and sometimes only the memory of Maria helped Anthony to cope. And when he remembered the maid who loved him, her advice came back, and he learned to take all his troubles to God in prayer. But the blows the boys often landed on him were nothing to the blow that came in a letter from home bringing the news that his only real friend had died. Maria, he knew, was with Jesus, but how he longed that she was still with him and that he was no longer in that terrible school. Because Maria was dead, the last thing Anthony wanted to do was to go back home for the holidays.

When he was nine years old, in 1809, his father became the Earl of Shaftesbury, and the family moved out of London to St Giles, the family mansion house in Wimborne, Dorset. At least Anthony could escape from his father's anger in the land around the house. And he was always back on time for meals because in her will Maria had left him her gold watch. Although he lived to be an old man, and a famous one too, that was the watch he always carried.

Three years later, when he was twelve years old, Anthony was sent to Harrow, one of the most famous schools in England.

'I wonder what it'll be like,' he thought as he travelled there for the first time. 'It can't be any worse than prep school. Nothing could be worse than that.'

It wasn't worse; in fact it was far, far better. Soon he made friends, got to know his schoolmasters and settled down to a life that was better than any he had known before. But he never forgot the boy he had been.

'If I have children,' he often thought, 'I'll treat them as Maria treated me. I'll be kind to them, read stories to them and play with them too.' For a minute he tried to imagine his father reading him a story and playing a game with him, but he couldn't.

'What's that noise?' he wondered, as he walked near Harrow School one day. He went to find out and he wished he had not. When he turned a corner, he saw a funeral procession unlike any he'd ever seen before. It was a parish funeral - the dead man had left no money to pay for a coffin – and four drunks were staggering with the cheap coffin often nearly falling off their shoulders. And the songs they sang as they went along were unspeakable. Unable to take his eyes off the scene, the teenager followed the grotesque procession to the grave into which the coffin was tipped like rubbish.

'I don't know how I'll do it,' Anthony promised, 'but I'll do everything in my power to help poor people like that dead man.' As he walked back to school, he shivered at the memory of what he had seen.

Although the Earl wanted his son to go into the army, Anthony went to university, and by the time he was twenty-five years old he was a Member of Parliament.

'It's only by changing the law that things will get better for the poor,' he often said. 'That's the only reason I'm in Parliament.'

'Speaking up for the poor won't make you a fortune,' a friend who had been at university said. 'And it won't make you friends either.'

'I can hardly take in what you're saying,' Anthony told the man who came to see him.

'You're telling me that children as young as five work in factories and coal mines, sometimes for fifteen hours a day!'

His companion nodded. The Member of Parliament sat down, shaking his head in disbelief. 'But what can a child of five do in a coal mine?'

Taking a deep breath his visitor began. 'Let me tell you of a five-year-old girl I met, though she is small and looks even younger. She goes down the mine at four in the morning and is often there till five in the evening. All day she crouches in the pitch-black tunnel just inside a wooden door. When she hears the rattle of coal being brought along the tracks, she pulls the door open and lets it pass. And when it does, it is often pulled by a child not much older than she is. But they can't see each other in the black darkness.'

'But why so young?' Anthony asked.

'The tunnels are narrow and low,' the visitor explained. 'Only children and small women can crawl through them, and only half-starved ones at that.'

To the man's amazement he saw that his story had brought tears to Anthony's eyes. And he was even more amazed when he realised that the Member of Parliament was not ashamed of crying.

'Surely the factory children are better off than that,' Anthony said. 'At least they see the light of day.'

'There are windows in the mills,' his visitor admitted, 'not that the children who work there have time to look up and see them. For half the year they arrive at work in the dark and don't leave until it's dark again for they work the same long hours as the children who are down the mines. The machinery they work with is so loud that they can't hear anything over it and often, by the time they've grown up, they have very little hearing left.'

Anthony thought of his own children, of the long hours they played in the summer sunshine, of the fun and games he had with them. But his companion's story wasn't finished.

'By the end of the day these children are so exhausted that they sometimes have to be carried home, that's if they've survived the day.'

'What do you mean?' the Member of Parliament asked.

'Sadly, many are seriously injured, even killed, by the mill machinery. There is rarely anything done to prevent accidents, and they are too tired to take good care of themselves.'

Anthony shuddered. 'Thank you,' he said to the man. 'You have opened my eyes.'

The following Sunday Anthony was in church with his wife and children. As they sang a verse of a hymn, it was as though the kind man read the words for the very first time.

God gave the rich his riches,
He gave the poor his place;
And each where God has set him
Should sing his Father's praise.

He stopped singing. 'That's not true!' he thought. 'That's just not true! God doesn't want rich people to get richer and poor people to die of hunger. A loving God doesn't want rich children's rooms full of toys and poor children cowering down coal mines! From this day on I will work my heart out for children who are treated less well than animals.' Anthony's son wondered why his father had stopped singing.

Anthony spent years trying to have a law passed by Parliament that only allowed children to work for ten hours a day. Many Members of Parliament were mill owners or mine owners and they certainly didn't want that law to be passed. If it became law, they would have to employ more children, and that would cost them more money. They fought against the Bill every time it came to the House of Commons. But Anthony, who had not been loved as a child, loved the poor children with all his heart. He lost friends; he made enemies; but he struggled on. His father would have nothing to do with him, but his wife supported him all the way. Like Anthony she was a Christian and she too had a heart for children. Eventually, after many struggles, many prayers, and a great many tears, a law was passed.

'What's the most important thing you've done in your life?' one of his children asked Anthony. By then his father had died and he was the Earl of Shaftesbury. But these things were not important to him.

'Was it limiting children's working hours?' his daughter asked. Anthony thought before answering.

'I think,' he said, 'that what was even more important, was encouraging the Christian Church to see that God has not given some the right to be rich and left others to be forever poor. Only when Christians began to accept that, did they become interested in doing anything for the mill children and those who worked down the mines.'

'Is that why you support London City Mission?' asked his daughter.

'It certainly is. The mission was started because Christians saw what was happening to the poor. And it thrills my heart that its missionaries search the darkest corners of London to find those who most need their help, and those who most need Jesus. You see, my dear,' he concluded, 'at the beginning of this century the church was interested in the good folk who attended. It is now beginning to minister to those who are far outside.'

FACT FILE
The statue of Eros in Piccadilly Circus, London, was erected as a memorial to Lord Shaftesbury. However, the Mines Act of 1842 which forbade women, and boys and girls under ten years of age to be employed in coal mines is a more lasting and meaningful memorial. Shaftesbury also helped bring about improvements in health, education and the care of the mentally ill.

Keynote: Shaftesbury was singing a hymn one day when he realised that what he was singing was wrong. It is important when you read books written by people to ask, 'Is this true?' Use your own mind and God's Word to come to the right decision. What does God say about it? Shaftesbury knew that it was wrong to say that rich people were rich and poor people poor and that was that. God tells us to have mercy on the poor. Proverbs 14:31.

Think: Shaftesbury was often frightened as a little boy. However, he thought that you could only go to Jesus when you died. Jesus has promised, 'I am with you always.' Do you worry about the future? Are you frightened of bullies? Are you scared of going somewhere new? Cast your cares on God because he cares for you. Ask God to guide you. Ask him to show you who you should share your problems with. God has many people who love him and who are able and willing to help you.

Prayer: Lord Jesus, give me peace of heart and mind when I have troubles. Give me the strength of character to do the right thing and stand up for others. Help me to love and be obedient to you. May you be the most important person in my life ... the one I love most of all and the only one I worship. Amen.

Thomas Chalmers

Thomas and his older brother William stood on the shore watching six men row their fishing boat out of Anstruther harbour on the east coast of Scotland.

'There's a wind blowing up,' William said. 'They'd better stick close to the shore.'

'I suppose they've got to go where the fish are,' Thomas reasoned. 'And there's been little enough fish lately. They must be getting pretty desperate.'

'What makes you think that?' his brother asked.

'Just something I heard Father say,' Thomas explained. 'When we were coming out of church on Sunday, I heard him telling the elders that, unless the fish came in, there would be starving children in Anstruther.'

'We're lucky we're not among them,' William said. 'There'll be plenty on the table when we get home.'

'And there'll be a telling-off as well if we don't get a move on.'

The boys pushed their hands deep into their pockets and headed for home.

'Listen to the noise!' William laughed, as they reached their door.

Thomas nodded. 'That's one reason I like the shore,' he said. 'It's the only place where there's peace to think!'

'What do you expect,' his brother teased, 'when you've got so many brothers and sisters?' His brother grinned. 'I don't mind the five older ones.'

'I should hope not,' laughed William, who was a year and a bit older than Thomas.

'It's the younger ones that make the noise.'

'I know what you mean,' his brother agreed. 'There are thirteen of us already and another one on the way. I wonder how many more are still to come.'

'None, I hope,' Thomas said. 'There's nowhere we can get peace to study in the whole house.'

William nearly split his sides laughing. 'Since when did that bother you?' he was able to ask eventually.

Thomas Chalmers grinned, pushed the door open and shouted above the noise, 'We're home, Mother. Is it teatime?'

There were bread and oatcakes, hard and soft cheese, a big pat of butter, a bowl of gooseberry jam and a jug of frothy milk on the table when Mr Chalmers said grace. And there were only crumbs when the family had finished the meal.

'Is it true that the fishing's bad?' William asked his father, before they rose from the table.

'Yes,' the man answered. 'And that's not good news for Anstruther. There will be children going to bed with nothing in their stomachs this evening. I hope you're all grateful to the Lord for what you've eaten. It's not every family that can afford it.'

'Could we be poor one day, Papa?' one of the little girls asked.

Mr Chalmers smiled kindly at her. 'We're blessed by having money in the bank,' he explained. 'Poor folk only have what's in their pockets, and when that runs out, they go hungry.'

'Is there nothing we can do to help?' Thomas asked.

'Your mother and I do what we can,' his father said, 'and I hope you'll do that, too, when you grow up and have an income of your own.'

Thomas packed that thought away in his mind, picked up a ball and called for his brothers to come for a game.

Mrs Chalmers watched her sons from the window. She loved these summer evenings when the family was together, even windy ones when their ball went all over the place. 'It's strange,' she thought. 'Thomas is right in the middle of the family but he's the leader of them. Look at him now, keeping them all in order and deciding who should run for the ball when it's blown away. And I'm sure he's got intelligence, though he's not discovered how to work yet. He must have a good brain inside that huge head of his. And what a laugh he has!' She smiled at the thought. 'He can outlaugh, outrun, outplay and outwit most of the boys in the village. But they still get on with him for he's so easy-going.'

'What are you thinking about?' Mr Chalmers asked, seeing the smile that was playing on his wife's face. He nodded when she shared her thoughts. 'He is a grand lad,' the man said, 'but he'll need to pull his socks up and discover how to work. In fact,' he went on, knowing that what he was going to say would surprise his wife, 'I think he should go off to university with William in the autumn.'

The smile cleared from Mrs Chalmers' face. 'But he's not twelve yet,' she said.

'And William is only a year older,' her husband pointed out. 'If the pair of them go together, Thomas might settle down and work. His teacher says he's well able for it.'

A few months later, in the autumn of 1792, William and Thomas Chalmers began their studies at St Andrews University.

'Be sure to write,' their mother said, as she watched them go. William was thirteen, and his little brother was eleven years old.

When they went home for their first holiday, their father was anxious to know what they had learned. And while Thomas told him about maths which he loved, he didn't mention that his chief interests at university were the same as they had been at home – running, football and handball, and that he was getting quite a reputation for his handball. Somehow Thomas felt that was probably not what his father most wanted to hear!

'What do you want to do after you finish at the university?' a local fisherman asked Thomas during that holiday.

'I want to be a minister,' he said, as he had done for some years. 'I don't think I've ever wanted to be anything else.'

'But are you not learning other things that take your interest?' the man wondered.

'Oh yes,' Thomas told him. 'There's maths. I just love maths. But I can do that as well as be a minister.'

The fisherman, who was an elder in the church, wondered about the young Thomas. 'His parents are faithful Christians,' he

137

thought, watching Thomas's back as he strolled along the shore, 'but I don't think that Master Thomas knows the Lord Jesus yet, even though he wants to be a minister.'

When he was fifteen years old, Thomas Chalmers began to study for the ministry, and in 1803 he became minister of a church in his home county of Fife. Just as he thought as a boy, he combined being a minister with lecturing in maths at his old university. But a few years later he had to do some serious thinking when a brother and one of his sisters died and Thomas himself was ill for many months. It was as he was getting better that he realised his priorities had been all wrong. He wrote to a friend, 'I resolve to devote every talent and every hour to the defence and illustration of the gospel.' And that's just what he did.

In 1815, Thomas left Fife with his young wife Grace to become a minister in the great city of Glasgow.

'We have to do something for the children who live around the church,' he told his elders. 'Many of them know nothing about the Lord Jesus. And we need to visit everyone who lives in the area. I reckon that's over eleven thousand people.'

The elders gasped but agreed it had to be done.

'First things first,' their minister said, 'how do we go about reaching the children?'

The men talked about it, prayed about it and decided to arrange a Sunday evening school for them. There were thirteen at the first meeting. Two years later there were 1,200!

One Sunday, after he had returned home from the class, Thomas sat in front of the fire thinking. 'It's a strange thing,' he smiled at the memory. 'I remember William and I talking when we were boys, and I said I hoped that thirteen other children were all we would have in the family. And here we are with a family of 1,200 children in the church, all started off from a little group of thirteen. When I was young I thought thirteen was a terrible lot of children. How things change!'

'Are you aware, brothers,' Chalmers told the elders of his church, 'that many of the children who come to our classes can neither read nor write?'

The men nodded seriously. 'But what can we do about that?' the bravest of them asked, knowing that when their minister saw something needing to be done, he usually found a way to do it.

Thomas looked the man in the eye. 'We can open schools for them,' he said. 'God doesn't only care for the souls of these children; he's interested in every part of them, their education included.'

Some of the elders caught the vision right away, others took longer, but within quite a short time schools were set up for nearly 700 children.

If Chalmers' elders wondered what their minister would think of next, they didn't have long to wait. 'We must discuss the care of the poor,' he told the men at a church meeting.

'This city is full of poor people,' one elder thought. 'And anything we do will just be a drop in the ocean.' But he listened to what Thomas was saying, and even he began to catch his minister's vision as he heard what he had to say.

'At present,' Chalmers said, 'the poor are provided for from the poor rate levy. But if we think back to the Bible, we'll realise that collections for the poor should be made within the church and deacons should use that money to make sure that the really poor have what they need. Not only that, the deacons should know the people well and their families too, so they can help families care for their own instead of being dependent on others.'

'But surely that's not the job of the church,' one elder wondered aloud.

'But surely it is,' Thomas Chalmers boomed. 'Have you not read the Bible?'

'You couldn't have put another person into the church today,' Grace Chalmers told her husband after a special service in 1823. He smiled. 'When I was young, I used to wonder how many children could be packed into one house! But I discovered that as many as came could be fitted in somewhere.'

Suddenly Thomas looked serious. 'The church was built to hold 1,700,' he said, 'and it's reckoned that over 3,000 were there today, and all to say goodbye to us.'

There was a long silence before he continued. 'I'll miss the Glasgow people so much. I wouldn't leave unless I was sure it was God's will for me to lecture at university.'

His wife nodded her head. 'I know that,' she said. 'And I'll miss them too.'

Although Thomas Chalmers moved away, he didn't forget the people of Glasgow or the lessons he had learned as their minister. He remembered the poverty and sickness he had found in Glasgow's alleyways. He remembered the children who could neither read nor write, and the men who couldn't find work. He remembered mothers who starved themselves so that their children had bread to eat. And he knew that Christians should do something about it.

As the years passed from the 1820s through the 1830s to the early 1840s, and Chalmers became more and more well known, people began to listen to what he had to say and to take seriously the problems of the poor. It was as though the Church began to wake up; as though it rubbed its eyes and saw what Scotland was really like, then shook itself and did what it could to help.

But while good things were happening in the Church, there were things going on that worried Thomas Chalmers and a number of others.

'We just can't sit and let this happen,' he said to a minister friend, as they discussed the situation. 'Congregations should be able to choose their own ministers. Landlords have no right to put men in churches when the people don't want them!'

'I agree,' his friend replied. 'But what can we do about it?'

'We can pray,' Thomas announced. 'And we can ask God to guide us through the next General Assembly.'

When that large annual meeting of the Church of Scotland was held in May 1843, Chalmers and around 400 others who agreed with him, felt the right thing to do was to walk out. Having left the Assembly Hall, they gathered in another building where they established the Free Church of Scotland with Thomas Chalmers as its first Moderator.

'It's a sad time,' a young minister said, 'but it's an exciting one too.'

'Yes,' his friend agreed. 'There's a great sadness over Scotland, but a great opportunity is opening up.'

The two men didn't realise that Thomas Chalmers was walking behind them and could hear what they were saying.

'Yes, my good friends,' he said, drawing alongside them, 'it's an opportunity to do more than choose our own ministers. It's a God-given opportunity to be like the early church and to have a real concern for the people of Scotland.'

'That's something we've learned from you, Dr Chalmers,' the young man said.

'I don't know where you learned it,' he said. 'But just don't forget it. We won't be a Church worth the Christian name if we do.'

FACT FILE
School: In the United Kingdom in 1870, schools only taught reading, writing and arithmetic. In 1872 in Scotland you could be educated until you were thirteen. In 1914 more than 70,000 children spent half the day at school and the other half working in a factory. In 1944 free secondary education for all was provided.

Keynote: Thomas Chalmers did not have a saving faith in Jesus Christ when he started to study for the ministry. It was only after his illness and the death of his brother and sister that things changed. He realised that there was no point in preaching unless you preached about the forgiveness of sins that Jesus has made available by his death on the cross. That's what he meant when he said, 'I resolve to devote every talent and every hour to the defence and illustration of the gospel.'

Think: It is important to have a real concern for the people of your own country and area. Think about what it needs. Are there poor people who need help? What can you do? There are definitely people you know who do not know about the Lord Jesus. How about talking to them about what you learn at Church, Sunday school or youth group? You could start a prayer group to pray about your town or country.

 Prayer: Father God, please be with the people of my town and my country. May this land be a place which honours and obeys your Word. Be with those people who run the country and make decisions. May they be people who love you. Help the churches in my country to be worthy of the name of Jesus Christ. Help us all to obey your Word. Amen.

QUIZ

How much can you remember
about the ten boys who
made a difference?

Try answering these questions
to find out ...

Augustine of Hippo

1. Which continent did Augustine live in as a young boy?

2. What was Augustine's mother's name?

3. Which book of the Bible was Augustine reading when he became a Christian?

Jan Hus

4. In which city did Jan go to university?

5. Which English preacher did Jan Hus agree with?

6. What happened to Jan in Gottlieben Castle?

Martin Luther

7. What did Martin Luther's father work as?

8. What was Martin going to be before the thunderstorm?

9. Martin wrote a list of ways in which the Church wasn't obeying the Bible. How many points were on this list?

Ulrich Zwingli

10. Which country was Ulrich Zwingli from?

11. When Ulrich and some other men were at the printing house, what did the printer's wife bring them to eat?

12. Which German Reformer did Ulrich Zwingli admire?

William Tyndale

13. What language was used in churches when William was a young boy?

14. What language did William translate the Bible into?

15. What did Henry Phillips do to Tyndale?

Hugh Latimer

16. In which university did Hugh Latimer become a teacher in 1510?

17. What was the name of the other man who was sentenced to death alongside Hugh Latimer?

18. Who did Latimer pray for before he died?

John Calvin

19. Which of John Calvin's parents died when he was a young boy?

20. What did Calvin study in Paris?

21. Which city did Calvin eventually settle in?

John Knox

22. What was the name of the village in which John Knox was born?

23. What was the name of John's friend who was martyred?

24. Who became very angry with John Knox when he preached against the Mass?

Lord Shaftesbury

25. What was the name of the maid who looked after Anthony when he was a little boy?

26. What did Anthony become when he left university?

27. Name one of the missions that Anthony supported when he grew up.

Thomas Chalmers

28. What was the name of the fishing village that Thomas lived in as a boy?

29. What was the name of the city that Thomas went to work in, in 1815?

30. How many children came to the Sunday school after two years?

How well did you do?

Turn over to find out...

Answers:

1. Africa

2. Monica

3. Romans

4. Prague

5. Wycliffe

6. Imprisoned then killed

7. A miner

8. A lawyer

9. 95

10. Switzerland

11. Sausages

12. Martin Luther

13. Latin

14. English

15. Betrayed him

16. Cambridge

17. Mr Ridley

18. Queen Elizabeth I

19. His mother

20. Theology

21. Geneva

22. Haddington

23. George Wishart

24. Mary, Queen of Scots

25. Maria

26. A Member of Parliament

27. London City Mission

28. Anstruther

29. Glasgow

30. 1,200

Start collecting this series now!

Ten Boys who used their Talents:
ISBN 978-1-84550-146-4
Paul Brand, Ghillean Prance, C.S.Lewis,
C.T. Studd, Wilfred Grenfell, J.S. Bach,
James Clerk Maxwell, Samuel Morse,
George Washington Carver, John Bunyan.

Ten Girls who used their Talents:
ISBN 978-1-84550-147-1
Helen Roseveare, Maureen McKenna,
Anne Lawson, Harriet Beecher Stowe,
Sarah Edwards, Selina Countess of Huntingdon, Mildred Cable,
Katie Ann MacKinnon,
Patricia St. John, Mary Verghese.

Ten Boys who Changed the World:
ISBN 978-1-85792-579-1
David Livingstone, Billy Graham, Brother Andrew,
John Newton, William Carey, George Müller,
Nicky Cruz, Eric Liddell, Luis Palau,
Adoniram Judson.

Ten Girls who Changed the World:
ISBN 978-1-85792-649-1
Corrie Ten Boom, Mary Slessor,
Joni Eareckson Tada, Isobel Kuhn,
Amy Carmichael, Elizabeth Fry, Evelyn Brand, Gladys Aylward,
Catherine Booth, Jackie Pullinger.

Ten Boys who Made a Difference:
ISBN 978-1-85792-775-7
Augustine of Hippo, Jan Hus, Martin Luther,
Ulrich Zwingli, William Tyndale, Hugh Latimer,
John Calvin, John Knox, Lord Shaftesbury,
Thomas Chalmers.

SOME BOOKS IN THE
TRAILBLAZERS SERIES

For a full list of Trailblazers, please see our
website: www.christianfocus.com
All Trailblazers are available as e-books

Martin Luther: Reformation Fire
by Catherine Mackenzie

What made an ordinary monk become a catalyst for the Reformation in Europe in the 1500s? What were the reasons lying behind his nailing of 93 theses against the practice of indulgences to the door of the Schlosskirche in Wittenberg in 1517? Why was Martin Luther's life in danger? How did his apparent kidnapping result in the first ever New Testament translated into the German language? Discover how a fresh understanding of the Scriptures transformed not only his own life but had a huge impact upon Europe.

ISBN: 978-1-78191-521-9

CHRISTIAN FOCUS PUBLICATIONS

Christian Focus | Christian Heritage | CF4K | Mentor

Christian Focus Publications publishes books for adults and children under its four main imprints: Christian Focus, CF4K, Mentor and Christian Heritage. Our books reflect our conviction that God's Word is reliable and Jesus is the way to know him, and live for ever with him.

Our children's publication list includes a Sunday School curriculum that covers pre-school to early teens, and puzzle and activity books. We also publish personal and family devotional titles, biographies and inspirational stories that children will love.

If you are looking for quality Bible teaching for children then we have an excellent range of Bible stories and age-specific theological books.

From pre-school board books to teenage apologetics, we have it covered!

Find us at our web page:
www.christianfocus.com

CF4•K
Because you're never
too young to know Jesus